Teach Yourself Grammar
A Clear and Concise Guide with Practice Problems

Paul Battles, PhD

Pandion Press
2016

For Dominique and Perry

Preface

A few years ago, when my son was learning grammar in school, he was frustrated at not being able to understand the subject. Since I had been teaching courses in linguistics and grammar at the college level for more than twenty years, I offered to help him.

As I read through his textbook, I was surprised at how outdated the information in it was. During the past fifty years, our understanding of language has grown by leaps and bounds. Just as the theories of relativity and quantum mechanics revolutionized the field of physics in the early twentieth century, breakthroughs in linguistic theory have transformed our understanding of grammar since the 1960s. However, none of these insights are reflected in school grammars, which have remained virtually unchanged since the second World War. In fact, if you look up some grammar textbooks from the early 1800s – you can find them on Google books – you'll see that very little has changed since then, either.

When students take a college-level linguistics class, they are amazed at the difference in what they learn there and what they've been taught about language before. They always ask why grammar isn't taught this way in school, which is a great question.

Imagine being a student in high school physics and learning only Newtonian physics, with no mention quantum mechanics or general relativity, only to be introduced to these theories in college. Then further imagine that even the course in Newtonian physics hadn't received an update since the 1960s, and no thorough-going revision for a hundred and fifty years before that. I think we can all agree that this would be a very bad way to organize a school curriculum in physics! However, it's exactly the way we approach the teaching of grammar.

When I explained all of this to my son, he asked to learn "the up-to-date stuff." At that time, he was finishing eighth grade. After a stint in school, he had decided to return to home schooling for high school. I thought it would be fun for the two of us to study grammar together, so I agreed.

As it happened, at the same time I was looking for a new textbook for my college course on grammar. Prices on these books had sky-rocketed – a trend that shows no signs of slowing down – so that they all cost more than $100, and most closer to $200. (Textbook publishers know a captive audience when they see one.) I also wanted to quit teaching out of 700-page tomes. When it comes to explaining grammar, less is more; students do best when the necessary information is set out clearly but briefly, allowing them to get right to the practical applications. Chapters should be short enough to be read in a single sitting, with plenty of exercises to practice each concept.

Although I searched long and hard for such a book, none turned up. So, I decided to write my own.

In doing so, I had in mind three audiences: self-learners; home-schoolers; and students, including those in my college grammar course. The book's first actual reader was my son, who used a draft to study grammar during the second semester of his sophomore year in high school. He gave me lots of suggestions for how to improve the book. I then used a revised draft as textbook for my college class on English grammar, and the students in that class, too, offered lots of further feedback, which I used to produce the final version of the book, which you're now reading.

Since this grammar is intended for self-learners and students, it's important to get as much feedback about it as possible, and I will continue to use these suggestions to improve future editions of it. (If you would like to send feedback, I'd like to hear from you at `https://teachyourselfgrammar.wordpress.com/contact/`).

Who this book is for

This book assumes no prior knowledge of grammatical rules and terminology. However, it is not intended as an ESL (English as a Second Language) text. It also uses North American English as the basis for its discussions.

I've tried to keep the individual chapters short enough to be read in a single sitting. Most should take between thirty minutes and an hour to complete (including exercises).

How to use this book

This book contains thirty chapters: twenty-seven lessons and three unit reviews. If you're pressed for time, you could work your way through the whole book in thirty days. Of course, you can go at whatever pace works best for you. In my semester-long college course, we cover two chapters per week. If you read one chapter per week, the book would take an academic year to complete.

Each chapter also contains a list of key terms, questions, and exercises. (The first time a term is introduced, it will be in SMALL CAPS.) The exercises are designed to help you master the material. You can do as many of these as you like; the more you do, the better will be your grasp of the concepts. I do recommend that you memorize all of the key terms. In the age of Google, memorization may seem like an obsolete skill, but it's vital for mastering grammar. Because these terms are cumulative, you should periodically practice recalling all of them, including ones from earlier units. If you have only a vague understanding of what a *noun* is, you will struggle with *determiners, adjectives,* and *pronouns,* to say nothing of *noun phrases, subjects, objects,* and *complements.* Quizlet, a terrific flash-card tool that allows you to study material in several different ways, has study sets that I've created specifically created for this book. You'll find them at `https://quizlet.com/`

`hrpb/folders/teach-yourself-grammar`. Drilling these sets is a great way to learn the key terms.

The companion website for this book, which you can find at `https://teachyourselfgrammar.wordpress.com`, has a variety of resources, including the answers to the exercises in every lesson, all the diagrams and tables included in this book as a separate pdf, links to the Quizlet sets, and more. All are free and downloadable with a click.

Again, if you have suggestions, comments, or questions, I'd like to hear from you at `https://teachyourselfgrammar.wordpress.com/contact`.

Contents

III. Clauses   149

Part I.

Words

1. The Nature of Grammar

The GRAMMAR of a language is the set of rules through which it combines words into larger units. Such units include the CLAUSE, a group of words that contains a *subject* and a *predicate* (in *Charlie smiled*, the subject is *Charlie* and the predicate *smiled*), and the PHRASE, a word or group of words that functions as a grammatical unit but does not contain both subject and predicate. Historically, there have been three major approaches to the study of grammar: pedagogical, prescriptive, and descriptive.

PEDAGOGICAL GRAMMARS focus on teaching beginning students the rudiments of a formal, literary language. The first books of grammar in the Western tradition taught literary Greek and Latin to students whose everyday speech would have been the "common" (Greek: *koine*, Latin: *vulgar*) variety of the language. Because Latin was the language of learning in medieval and early modern Europe, handbooks of Latin grammar like Donatus' *Art of Grammar* also deeply influenced the study of English grammar. For example, the eight "parts of speech" familiar from modern pedagogical grammars – nouns, pronouns, adjectives, adverbs, verbs, conjunctions, prepositions, and interjections – derive from Latin grammar books. Pedagogical grammars are typically written for students or non-native speakers of a language.

PRESCRIPTIVE GRAMMARS present rules, often formulated as a list of do's and don'ts, that aim to improve the reader's use of language. Historically, prescriptive grammar is closely related to pedagogical grammar, which, as already noted, taught students how to write literary Greek and Latin. Along with his grammar, Donatus also created a list of twelve errors in usage (*barbarisms* and *solecisms*), and similar lists are commonplace in English prescriptive grammars (e.g., *split infinitives* and *dangling participles*). Because English has no body of experts comparable to the *Académie française* – the acknowledged authority on matters of French usage, vocabulary, and grammar – prescriptivists often present conflicting lists of do's and don'ts. "Do's and don'ts" itself is a good example. Some experts claim that this should be written *dos and donts*, others *do's and don'ts*, and still others *do's and don't's*. Today, books with a prescriptive outlook are written mostly by journalists for general readers.

DESCRIPTIVE GRAMMARS describe language as it is used by typical native speakers of a language. Descriptive grammar is associated with *linguistics*, the scientific study of language. Like other scientists, linguists aim for objectivity in their analysis. Most linguists are university professors, editors of language reference works, or both. Their books are written primarily for other linguists and for advanced university students.

Despite their obvious differences, all three branches of language study – pedagogical, prescriptive, and descriptive – draw on the same traditions, and each has strengths and weaknesses. Pedagogical and prescriptive grammars are useful for individuals who want to improve their language skills, enabling them to succeed in school and in the workplace. Unfortunately, these books' advice is often outdated, inaccurate, and subjective. Descriptive grammars, on the other hand, are based on the best and latest research about language. However, they offer little practical information to help students become better speakers and writers of English; they are also typically written for an academic audience.

This book combines the best of all three approaches. Since descriptive grammar contains the most accurate information about how language works, it informs everything this book discusses. Having taught grammar for more than two decades, I will also share the best strategies, tips, and tricks from the pedagogical tradition, while also debunking ones that don't work. Finally, for readers interested in improving their writing, notes on usage detail various prescriptive rules and discuss their usefulness.

The remainder of this chapter will outline a few general principles that will help to contextualize the study of English grammar.

Language is infinitely creative

Many animals have ingenious systems for communicating. Some honeybees perform intricate dances that alert other members of their hive to nearby sources of pollen. However, no known animal communication system comes even remotely close to the complexity of the human language, which can convey an infinite number of messages about an infinite number of topics. (Bees converse only about a single subject: pollen.) The principle of infinite creativity extends to a number of different aspects of language. Though an individual may have a vocabulary of only a few thousand words, there is no limit to how these words can be combined. Moreover, the English alphabet has just 26 letters, but these can spell a theoretically limitless number of words. Linguists call this principle INFINITE USE OF FINITE MEANS.

Language is creative because people are creative. As we invent new things, like tablets and cell phones, we need new words to talk about them. Sometimes, we simply re-purpose already existing words. The word *tablet* existed before the advent of the Apple iPad, but now it has the additional meaning of "handheld computer." At other times, we create new words, like *selfie*, whose first recorded use was in 2002.

Language continually changes

Linguists have studied many languages, but they have only discovered one kind that does not change: dead ones. All living languages constantly change.

Consider the following English statements: *Hwaet! We Gar-Dena in gear-dagum theod-cyninga thrymm gefrunon, hu tha aethelingas ellen cythdon!* Your response may be, "That's not English!" On the contrary. These are the opening lines of a masterwork of English literature, *Beowulf.* This poem was written over a thousand years ago, around 750 CE. Since that time, English has changed so much as to be become an almost entirely different language. Students of OLD ENGLISH – English as it was spoken and written from about 450 to 1100 – study its vocabulary and grammar just as they would that of a foreign language. A word-for-word translation of this passage would look something like this: *Listen! We about the Spear-Danes in days long ago, about the clan-kings' might, have heard, how those princes great deeds performed.* Whereas modern English indicates grammatical relationships mostly through word order, Old English does so through word endings. For example, the *-a* in *Gar-Dena* and *theod-cyninga* marks these words as possessive plurals, so we would translate them *of the Spear-Danes* and *of the clan-kings.* Native speakers of Old English would have had no difficulty deciphering the scrambled word order, but a modern translation has to rearrange the words. An idiomatic translation of these lines would look something like this: *Listen! We have heard about the might of Danish kings in days long ago, and about the greet deeds they performed.*

With a bit of help, you can decipher a few of the words in the lines cited above. For example, the initial *g-* in *gear-dagum* is pronounced like "y." *(Y)ear* evolved into the word *yore*, meaning "long ago," and *dagum* is an Old English form of *days*, so *gear-dagum* literally means "in yore-days," or "in days long ago." Other words, like *theod* ("tribe," "clan," "nation") and *thrymm* ("might," "glory"), have essentially died out. The compound *theod-cyninga*, "of the clan-kings," sounds odd, but it just means "about the [Danish] kings." *Cyning* is the Old English word that gives us modern *king*.

Considering how much English has changed since the days of *Beowulf*, it doesn't make sense to treat it – or any living language – as a fixed system with rules that will always stay the same. Modern American English is still evolving as well. We don't notice these changes because they happen slowly, but even slow changes add up over time. One example of a recent change involves the pronunciation of the vowel sounds in *horse* and *hoarse*. In most parts of the United States, these words are now pronounced identically; in the 1940s, they were not. The same holds true for the initial consonant sound in *witch* and *which*.

Because the English language is always changing, its rules of grammar and principles of usage change as well. In the *Beowulf* poet's day, it was common to use double negatives like *not none*. They were used to intensify; *not none* means *absolutely none*. Many languages today use double negatives in this way.

We learn language from those with whom we interact

By the time most children enter school, they already speak fluently. Thus, we do not learn language in school but by communicating with those closest to us. Usually, we model our speech on that of our family and friends. If they use expressions like *I didn't see nothing*, so do we.

As will be explained in more detail in chapter 28, English has three levels of style: informal, middle, and formal. The informal style, which is used in everyday conversation, permits expressions such as *I didn't see nothing*, whereas the middle and formal styles do not. For convenience's sake, we can use *formal written English* as a short-hand for the written form of the middle and formal styles.

Double negatives like *didn't see nothing* aren't "bad grammar." They are dialectal, ethnic, or socio-economic variations in the informal style. In other words, if you say *I didn't see nothing*, you are revealing something about your background; perhaps you are Southern, or African American, or from a blue-collar neighborhood.

Value judgments about language are really value judgments about people. For example, the statement *"I didn't see nothing" is ignorant* really means *I believe that people who say "I didn't see nothing" are ignorant*. Particular usages in spoken English, like dropping sounds at the end of a word – like saying *goin'* for "going" – are often condemned as lazy. If this were true, what would we make of the way French people pronounce words like *beaux* ("bo")? They drop not just one sound but several. Should we conclude that all French people are lazy? Surely not! It is equally unsafe to conclude anything about an English-speaking person's work ethic by how he or she pronounces "going." *Goin'* is simply an informal pronunciation.

Double negatives or *g*-dropping, then, do not violate the rules of English, but they indicate an informal stylistic register. The middle and formal styles would prefer *I didn't* (or *did not*) *see anything* and *going*.

No one is bad at grammar

Many people believe that they have "bad grammar." Unless they suffer from brain trauma, a mutation in the FOXP2 gene, or a similar (extraordinarily rare) condition, this is simply not true.

Consider the implications of the principle that we learn language from our care-givers and friends. If they speak a variety of English that diverges from the standard, then that is what we learn. Therefore, our grammar is not defective; we have simply learned some grammatical rules that differ from ones employed by the middle and formal styles.

At this point, it is worth pausing to consider the ORIGIN OF STANDARD LANGUAGE VARIETIES. Standard varieties are usually based on the dialect of a particularly important area, especially one home to influential writers. For example, modern Italian is based on a variation of the Tuscan dialect. The leading city of Tuscany, Florence, was home to the great writers Dante Alighieri, Giovanni Boccaccio, and Francesco Petrarch. Though they also wrote in Latin, each helped pioneer the use of Italian in literature. Standard Italian was based on the language these writers used in their works.

The standard form of most languages derives from a formal, literary version of that language. Even in Tuscany, ordinary Italians did not use the language of Dante's *Divine Comedy*. In fact, one reason Dante, Boccaccio, and Petrarch were so revered by their contemporaries is that their language was extraordinary; they were considered to have purified and embellished everyday language, transforming it into a language that could displace Latin as vehicle for discussing serious topics in a sophisticated way. With the advent of mass schooling and mass media, this literary language became the basis for education and communication.

In the U.S., the region whose language is closest to the standard is the North Midlands, an area in the center of the country with few truly distinctive forms. This lack of regionally marked forms makes the North Midlands dialect acceptable to the majority of Americans, which is important to a nation that prides itself on being a melting-pot of cultures. Natives of different parts of the country, such as the South or the Northeast, are often judged to have "bad grammar." Again, this is inaccurate. What such judgments reveal are regional biases. If you can communicate fluently, you have mastered the grammar of the particular variety you know.

"Knowing" grammar

One can be an expert at English grammar without knowing any grammatical terms. Children who have no notion of concepts like *subject* or *predicate* have no difficulty forming sentences like *Daddy smiled.*

Part of the confusion between KNOWLEDGE *of* GRAMMAR and KNOWLEDGE *about* GRAMMAR comes from the term itself. *Grammar* can refer to the set of rules through which a language combines words into larger units (the definition offered above), to the study of these rules, or even to a book about these rules. Knowledge *of* grammar means being able to speak a language, but knowledge *about* grammar means being able to name, describe, and analyze grammatical processes. Knowledge *of* grammar is learned intuitively, whereas knowledge *about* grammar requires active study.

As a sub-field of linguistics, grammar has its own terminology and its own analytical tools. In this respect, grammar is no different from math, biology, or other subjects.

A note on usage

As mentioned above, linguistics has moved away from the traditional, prescriptive approach to grammar. That does not mean that the basic goal of the prescriptivism – to use language more effectively– is wrong. However, having defined grammar as the set of rules through which a language combines words into larger units, we can see that prescriptivism does not aim to "improve one's grammar." Rather, it provides "prescripts" – guidelines – for better USAGE, the conventions that govern how language is used in formal contexts, especially writing. Studying grammar is a great way to improve one's knowledge of these conventions.

Terms, Questions, and Exercises

GRAMMAR, CLAUSE, PHRASE, PEDAGOGICAL GRAMMAR, PRE-SCRIPTIVE GRAMMAR, DESCRIPTIVE GRAMMAR, INFINITE USE OF FINITE MEANS, OLD ENGLISH, ORIGINS OF STANDARD LANGUAGE VARIETIES, KNOWLEDGE *of* GRAMMAR, KNOWLEDGE *about* GRAMMAR, USAGE.

1. Describe the differences between pedagogical, prescriptive, and descriptive grammar. What are some strengths and weaknesses of each approach?

2. Using common words, make up a sentence that you've never spoken or written before. How does this sentence illustrate the principle of "infinite use of finite means"?

3. "With the advent of the printing press and mass communication, language change has essentially stopped." Is this an accurate statement?

4. You have a friend who claims she is "bad at grammar." She speaks like everyone else you know. What are some reasons why she might believe that she is "bad at grammar"? To what extent is this statement probably misleading?

5. What is the difference in knowledge *of* grammar and knowledge *about* grammar?

6. What is "usage"? How does this term apply to prescriptive grammar?

2. Word Class

Language is modular, with smaller units combining to form larger ones: sentences are made up of clauses; clauses of phrases; and phrases of words. As we learned in chapter 1, the rules of grammar describe how to combine simpler structures into more complex ones. Therefore, we will begin our discussion with the smallest structure, the word.

You probably remember learning about *parts of speech* in school. Linguists call these *lexical categories* or *word classes*; we will use the latter term. Words belonging to a particular WORD CLASS share grammatical properties, specifically in SYNTAX (word order), MORPHOLOGY (word structure) and SEMANTICS (meaning).

Traditional grammars define word class by meaning alone, as in the following examples:

A *noun names a person, place, or thing.*

A *verb expresses action.*

Although these definitions are not incorrect, they are incomplete and difficult to apply.

Many nouns, such as *love, nationhood*, or *mileage*, name neither persons, places, or things, but abstractions. For this reason, some teaching grammars offer an expanded the definition: *A noun names a person, place, thing, <u>or idea</u>.* However, an "idea" is very difficult to define: *red, green, destroy, rescue, above*, and *below* could all be said to be "ideas," but they are not nouns. In short, the expanded definition of nouns is more inclusive than the shorter one, but it is also more ambiguous.

Likewise, many verbs do not express actions. In *She seems ill*, the verb *seems* indicates a state (illness). Again, teaching grammars often offer expanded definitions, such as *Verbs ex-*

13

press actions, events, or states of being. This does cover a wider range of cases, but not all. For instance, in *Sarah has a nice car*, *has* indicates ownership, not an action. Again, the expanded definition also creates potential for confusion. Doesn't *illness* describe a state of being, and *foreclosure* an event? These words are nouns, not verbs.

Moreover, many words can play different roles in a sentence, depending on context. Teaching grammars recognize this in a very few cases, creating categories like the *gerund*, a verb form that ends in *-ing* and acts like a noun, but in fact most words, not just a few, can fulfill multiple roles in a sentence. *Like*, which describes various forms of affinity, is a true word-class chameleon, taking on no less than seven different roles; it can function as a noun (*his likes and dislikes*), an adjective (*of like mind*), a verb (*I like pizza*), a preposition (*places like this*), and – in informal speech or writing – a conjunction (*I felt like I had died*), an adverb (*she's quiet like*), and an interjection (*He's, like, friendly*). Words that can belong to several classes are the rule, not the exception.

Words that change word classes undergo a FUNCTIONAL SHIFT. There are many reasons why words shift classes. For one, it is more efficient to re-use the same word than to create a new one; if the word *down* typically describes a direction (an adverbial function), why not create a corresponding verb that means *to lower or cause something to be lowered*? Language is also inherently creative, especially in coining slang expressions; one example is *I'm down with that*, an expression popularized by the television show *Buffy the Vampire Slayer*. When they are first coined, most slang expressions are considered non-standard, but many eventually become acceptable in any context, including *fan, fun, mob*, and many others.

Due to the prevalence of function shifts in English, it is helpful to distinguish a between a word's *form* and its *function*. FORM simply means appearance, in this case the class to which one would assign a particular word in the absence of context. For instance, the word *green* typically describes the color of an object, and it can also be compared (*greener, greenest*); therefore, in *form* it is an adjective. A word's FUNCTION – the role it plays – can only be determined by context. If someone is playing golf *on a green*, *green* is used like a noun. Today, a frequent topic of discussion is how to *green a workplace*, that is, how to make it conform with ecological principles (a sense first recorded in 1984); here *green* functions as a verb.

So far, we have concentrated on explaining the inadequacy of the traditional definitions of various word classes. How, then, can these be improved? By considering all three properties that play a role in word class – syntax, morphology, and semantics – rather than just semantics alone.

Content words and function words

All words belong to one of just two grammatical categories: content words and function words. As the name implies, CONTENT WORDS convey meaning. Whatever the topic that we want to communicate about, we could not do it without content words. By contrast, FUNCTION WORDS express relationships; they act like grammatical glue, allowing us to build larger structures out of simpler ones.

The category of content words includes *nouns* and *verbs*, which are the most common words, as well as *adjectives* (which most commonly modify nouns) and *adverbs* (which most commonly modify verbs).

The category of function words includes *determiners, pronouns, prepositions, conjunctions,* and *interjections*. Determiners, such as *the*, signal nouns (*the tree*). Pronouns, meanwhile, usually take the place of nouns. Prepositions are used to create *prepositional phrases*, which act like adjectives or adverbs. Conjunctions join together smaller units of all kinds – words, phrases, and clauses – into larger ones. Interjections, like *Ha!*, most often imitate sounds.

Because English sees a constant influx of new nouns, verbs,

adjectives, and adverbs, these classes are said to be OPEN. The function word classes, to which few if any words are being added, are said to be CLOSED.

Morphology

Many words announce their membership in a particular word class through their internal structure. All words are composed of one or more MORPHEMES, the minimal units of word meaning. When linguists study *morphology*, they examine the rules or principles of word formation; this term can also describe a particular word's structure.

There are two basic types of morphemes, roots and affixes. The ROOT provides the basic meaning of a word; all words must have at least one root. Some roots are FREE, meaning that they can occur on their own, while others are BOUND, meaning that they can not. In English, most *bound roots* are loan words from other languages. The bound root *ceive* occurs in words like *conceive, deceive, perceive,* and *receive,* which were all borrowed from French. The French words, in turn, derive from Latin. *Receive* originally comes from *re-* ("back") and *capere* ("to take"), that is, "to take something (back) into one's possession." The root *ceive* never occurs on its own, and is therefore *bound*.

Whereas roots provide the basic meaning of a word, an AFFIX provides additional information; it is always attached ("affixed") to one or more other morphemes. A PREFIX attaches before other morphemes, a SUFFIX after them. Affixes that are used to *derive* new words from already existing ones are called DERIVATIONAL morphemes. By contrast, INFLECTIONAL morphemes do not create new words, but provide grammatical information about the structures to which they attach. Inflectional morphemes always come at the very end of a word, after both roots and any other suffixes.

Let's take a look at an example. Since morphemes are the

minimal units of meaning, morphemic analysis breaks words down into their smallest units of meaning. Since all words have at least one root, it is a good idea to first identify the root. For example, the word *bakers* contains the root *bake*. *Bake* cannot be broken down into smaller units like *ba-* and *-ke*; although many words contain these sounds – *bar*, *bat*, *bay*, *cake*, *flake*, *shake*, and so on – *ba-* and *-ke* are not units of meaning, because the words they form have no common underlying meaning. Therefore, *bake* is a root. Because it can stand on its own, it is a *free* root. The remainder of the word, *-(e)rs*, is composed of two morphemes, *-(e)r* and *-s*. The suffix *-(e)r* occurs in many nouns formed from action words: a *baker* is someone who *bakes*, a *driver* is someone who *drives*, a *roller* is something that *rolls*, a *cutter* is something that *cuts*, and so on. Because it forms a new word – *bake* and *baker* being different things – *-er* is a *derivational* suffix. Finally, the *-s* provides information about how many bakers there are: more than one. Since *-s* adds only grammatical information (it is the *plural* form of the noun) and does not form a different word, it is an inflectional suffix. Because inflections always go at the end of words, the word is *bakers*, not **bakeser*. (Throughout this book, non-grammatical forms are marked with an asterisk.)

A knowledge of morphology is helpful because many morphemes signal word class. For example, most words ending in the derivational suffixes *-able*, *-ful(l)*, *-ish*, or *-y* – such as *quotable*, *helpful*, *stylish*, and *funny* – are adjectives. This rule is not infallible, for *-ish* also appears in many verbs, like *admonish*, *demolish*, *establish*, *perish*, and *replenish*. (Adjective-forming *-ish* comes from Old English *-isc*, while verb-forming *-ish* derives from French *-iss-*.) In other words, derivational suffixes can provide clues about a word's likely class, though we must always take care to verify this through other means.

Inflectional morphemes provide even more valuable clues about word class. Modern English has only eight inflectional morphemes: two for nouns, plural *-s* (*bakers*) and possessive *-'s / s'* (*baker's*); two for adjectives, comparative *-er* (*greater*) and superlative *-est* (*greatest*); and four for verbs, third person singular *-s* (*mows*), past tense *-ed* (*mowed*), present participle *-ing* (*mowing*), and past participle *-n*/*-ed* (*mown*). Because we'll refer to them throughout this book, you should commit this list to memory.

Remembering inflectional morphemes and their associated word class is also the best way to distinguish inflectional and derivational suffixes. Any suffix that is not inflectional must be derivational. When memorizing the inflectional morphemes, take note of its function, because some suffixes can be either derivational or inflectional depending on context. For instance, *-er* is derivational in *baker* but inflectional in *finer*. We can see that the *-er* in *baker* is derivational because it creates a different word (the verb *bake* becomes *baker*, a noun), whereas in *finer* it indicates the comparative degree of the adjective *fine*. (It may be helpful to note that, as with *-ish*, the different forms of *-er* were originally distinct morphemes that came to be spelled identically. Comparative *-er* derives from Old English *-ra*, while derivational *-er* conflates Old English *-ere*, Old French *-ier*, and Latin *-ar* /*-arius*.)

A note on usage

Some words can have multiple derivational morphemes pertaining to the same class. For instance, *-ic* and *-al* are both adjective-forming morphemes – *authentic*, *eclectic*, *heroic*, *annual*, *final*, *moral* – but there are many words that combine both suffixes, such as *physical*, *radical*, and *typical*. In some closely related word pairs, one word ends in *-ic* and the other in *-ical*. Sometimes, the words have distinct meanings, as in *economic* ("relating to the economy") and *economical* ("money-saving") or *politic* ("prudent") and *political* ("pertaining to politics"). Frequently, however, the paired words have no clear-cut difference in meaning, as in *mythic* / *mythical*, *problematic* / *problematical*, and *ironic* / *ironical*. In such cases, it's best to avoid the *-ical* forms in favor of the simpler *-ic.*

Terms, Questions, and Exercises

WORD CLASS, SYNTAX, MORPHOLOGY, SEMANTICS, FUNC-
TION SHIFT, FORM, FUNCTION, CONTENT WORDS, FUNCTION
WORDS, OPEN WORD CLASSES, CLOSED WORD CLASSES, MOR-
PHEME, ROOT MORPHEME, FREE MORPHEME, BOUND MOR-
PHEME, AFFIX, PREFIX, SUFFIX, DERIVATIONAL MORPHEME,
INFLECTIONAL MORPHEME.

1. Traditional grammars define word class by meaning alone.
   Why is this not adequate? What other grammatical properties can help to define word class?

2. What is the difference between a word's *form* and its
   function? Give an example of a *function shift*.

3. What are the two broad categories into which all words
   can be divided?

4. What is a morpheme? List the individual morphemes
   comprising the words listed below. Describe each morpheme as either free or bound, then specify whether it
   is a root, a prefix, a derivational suffix, or an inflectional
   suffix. (For example: *banker's* consists of the free root
   bank, the derivational suffix *er*, and the inflectional suffix
   's.

   a) sleeping
   b) fantastic
   c) deer-hunter's
   d) disgracefully
   e) designated [hint: consider words like *sign*, *assign*,
      and *resign*]

19

5. The derivational suffix -en is often used to turn adjectives into verbs: *black + en = blacken*, "make black"; *red + (d)en = redden*, "make red"; *loose + en = loosen*, "make loose."

a) Give the corresponding verbs formed from the adjectives *bright*, *deep*, *sweet*, *tight*, and *white*.

b) List three more adjectives which add *-en* to become verbs.

c) Name five adjectives – similar to *gloom*, *green*, or *bitter* – which cannot be turned into verbs by adding *-en* (**gloomen*, **greenen*, **bitteren*).

d) Are the *-en* verbs *heighten*, *lengthen*, and *strengthen* formed from adjectives? (If we remove the suffix, what words remain? Are these adjectives?)

6. If you're writing about chess, would it be preferable to talk about *strategic* or *strategical* positioning of pieces? Why?

3. Nouns

Nouns are the most common words in English. *Noun* comes from Latin *nomen*, "name," which is why grammars often state that nouns "name" persons, places, things, or ideas. As discussed in the previous chapter, this definition requires sharpening. A fuller and more accurate understanding of the class emerges through an examination of its semantics, morphology, and syntax.

Let's start with the kinds of meaning conveyed by nouns. Some do refer to people (*Bob, manager*) or places (*mall, Oklahoma*). As mentioned in the previous chapter, "idea" is an imprecise term. The same holds true for "thing." Is a butterfly a thing? Is a dog? It is more accurate to replace the traditional definition's *things and ideas* with *beings, objects, and abstractions*. Finally, some nouns describe times (*noon, Tuesday*) or events (*the Reformation, Christmas*). Summing up, then, nouns refer to beings, objects, places, times, events, or abstractions.

Inflectional morphemes help to identify nouns. The class of nouns has two: plural -*s* and possessive -*'s*. Only nouns can take these. In other words, if you can add an -*'s* to the end of a word to indicate possession, that word must be a noun. The same is true of plural -*s*. As we'll see shortly, not all nouns can take the plural -*s*; however, all words that can *are* nouns. Also, many nouns have derivational suffixes, such as -*age*, -*ance*/-*ence*, -*ation*/-*(t)ion*, -*ee*, -*er*, -*hood*, -*ism*/-*ist*, -*(i)ty*, -*ment*, -*or*, and -*ship*. Some of these turn words of other classes into nouns; -*ity* and -*ness* generally turn adjectives into nouns: *complex* becomes *complexity*, *possible* becomes *possibility*, *good* becomes *goodness*, and *ready* becomes *readiness*.

Others turn one kind of noun into another: *friend* becomes *friendship*, *member* becomes *membership*, and so on.

Syntactically, nouns have two identifying features. First, all nouns can be modified by appropriate adjectives. In most cases, the adjective can proceed the noun, with or without determiner (*wild rice, the grey cat*). In those cases where such a usage sounds odd (*soothing tranquility*), the adjective can follow a form of the verb *be* (*Tranquility is soothing*). Second, many nouns are preceded by *determiners* like *a, an,* or *the*; in fact, determiners signal words that function as nouns. Just as not all nouns can be made plural, however, not all are accompanied by determiners (**the rice, *a tranquility*).

To sum up the semantic, morphological, and syntactic properties of the class, NOUNS refer to beings, objects, places, times, events, or abstractions (*semantics*). They can take the possessive -'s and, in many cases, plural -s (*morphology*). Nouns can be modified by appropriate adjectives, and are often preceded by a determiner (*syntax*).

Note that words having undergone a function shift into the category of nouns exhibit some noun-like behaviors when used as such, but not when used as members of other word classes. The noun *green* references places, objects, or (in the plural) plants, and can be used in expressions like *The green's surface is uneven* or *the yummy taste of greens*. The adjective form of *green* does not follow noun rules, forbidding expressions like **the greens pencils* or **the flowers are greens*. Context is the only way to decide a word's class in such cases.

Kinds of nouns

In describing how nouns behave, we can distinguish between *common* and *proper* nouns. PROPER NOUNS denote *specific* beings, objects, places, times, events, or abstractions, whereas COMMON NOUNS refer to *members of a class*. *Stockholm* names a unique place, whereas *a city* or *the city* describes a member of the class of cities. Proper nouns are only rarely preceded by determiners like *the, a,* or *an.* For example, one would not say **The Kennedy was assassinated* or **A Luxembourg is a small country.* Exceptions include certain titles, as in *Edward de Vere, the Earl of Oxford,* a few place names like <u>the</u> *Netherlands,* and the names of organizations such as <u>the</u> *Associated Press.*

There are reasons for these exceptions. When a proper noun has several members, it can take a determiner to specify which is being discussed. There have been many earls of Oxford, of which Edward de Vere was one. Though we would not say *The Kennedy was assassinated,* a statement such as *A Kennedy was assassinated* makes better sense, meaning that "a member of the Kennedy family was assassinated." For other proper nouns preceded by "the," this determiner has really become part of the name. *The Netherlands,* a country informally also known as Holland, is a descriptive name that literally means *the nether [=low-lying] lands*; much of the country's territory lies below sea level. (Holland is also one of *the Low Countries.*) Likewise, the "the" in *The Associated Press* is part of the corporation's title. To confirm that the determiner functions as part of a title, we can try substituting a different determiner, like *a / an.* Expressions like **a Netherland* or **an Associated Press* sound wrong, showing that the determiner *the* has become part of the names *The Netherlands* and *The Associated Press.* By convention, proper nouns are capitalized.

We can also distinguish between *countable* and *uncountable* nouns (also called *count* and *mass* nouns). If a noun is COUNT-ABLE, it names something that is discrete and can therefore be enumerated, such as *two chairs, three weddings,* or *four promotions.* If it is UNCOUNTABLE, it names something that is not discrete and therefore cannot be enumerated, like **two milks, *three electricities,* or **four serenities.* Recipes often contain lists of uncountable nouns: *oil, water, milk, flour, sugar, salt, butter, vanilla extract, baking powder, baking soda, yeast,* and so on. Uncountable nouns have three morphological and syntactic properties: they are typically not found in the plural form (*oils*), counted (*two waters*), or preceded by the determiner *a(n)* (*a yeast*). Count nouns, on the other hand, *can* be pluralized, counted, and preceded by a determiner (*two eggs*, *an egg*).

Many nouns can switch from uncountable to countable in particular contexts. For example, in a chemistry lab we might well discuss several different salts (*common salt, ionic salt, alkali salt*, and so on) or oils (*vegetable oil, mineral oil*, and *volatile oil*). As we have already noted in our discussion of proper nouns, when discussing "kinds of" or "instances of" a normally uncountable noun, we often make it countable. Most abstractions make the switch with relative ease. When we refer to it as a general principle, *liberty* is uncountable, but we can also speak about particular *liberties*. Likewise, proper nouns are usually uncountable, except when they refer to instances of something that share the same name, as in *I know three Bobs* or *I love Fridays*. There are some nouns, however, that ordinarily cannot be pluralized (*informations, *satisfactions, *advices*).

Nominals

Some structures do not contain nouns but exhibit noun-like behavior; they are nouns in *function* but not in *form*. We will refer to these as NOMINALS. For instance, in the sentence *I wanted to laugh*, the phrase *to laugh* acts like a noun; we could complete *I wanted (something)* with many typical nouns, such as *water*. Nominals can play any noun role, and they vary in complexity from single words to lengthy constructions such as *I wanted to make you aware of the fact that such behavior will under no circumstances ever be tolerated by this company*; the basic structure remains *I wanted (something)*. Perhaps the most commonly occurring nominals are *-ing* words and phrases. (The different kinds of nominals will be discussed in chapters 16-17 and 22).

A note on usage

Turning a word of a different class into a noun is NOMINALIZA-TION. There is nothing wrong with nouns derived from other classes; we could hardly get by without them. However, excessive nominalization makes writing wordy, especially when a phrase's "action" is moved from the verb to the noun. Such sentences can often be improved by undoing the nominalization. For instance, in *We conducted an evaluation of the situation*, *evaluation* is the nominalized form of *evaluate*; thus, we could write *We evaluated the situation*. Instead of writing *She made an intervention*, we could simply say *She intervened*.

Terms, Questions, and Exercises

NOUN, PROPER NOUN, COMMON NOUN, COUNTABLE NOUN, UNCOUNTABLE NOUN, NOMINAL, NOMINALIZATION.

1. How do teaching grammars define nouns? Why is this inadequate?

2. Name the semantic, morphological, and syntactic properties of nouns.

3. Name five nouns formed with the suffix *-ation*.

4. Identify each noun in the following passage: *It was a dark and stormy night; the rain fell in torrents—except at occasional intervals, when it was checked by a violent gust of wind which swept up the streets (for it is in London that our scene lies), rattling along the housetops, and fiercely agitating the scanty flame of the lamps that struggled against the darkness.* (Edward Bulwer-Lytton opens his 1830 novel *Paul Clifford* with these often imitated and even more frequently parodied words.)

5. Revise each of the sentences below to remove unnecessary nominalization:

   a) Copernicus made the determination that the earth revolves around the sun.

   b) Caesar gave an exhortation to his troops to fight bravely.

   c) We came to the realization that the game would end in a draw.

4. Adjectives and Determiners

Adjectives and determiners play similar grammatical roles; they also differ in some important ways.

Adjectives

The class of adjectives is *open*. New adjectives are continually being added to the English language. For example, in the early 2000s, the comedian Stephen Colbert popularized the adjective *truthy*, meaning "having the appearance of being true." The corresponding noun, *truthiness*, was named "Word of the Year" for 2005 by the American Dialect Society.

Semantically, ADJECTIVES primarily serve to modify a noun or nominal, qualifying, specifying, or otherwise altering its meaning. The noun *shoes* could be modified by different adjectives such as *new*, *old*, *shiny*, *dirty*, *red*, and *brown* (*new shoes*, *red shoes*), or even by combinations like *shiny new shoes* or *dirty old brown shoes*. Depending on context, the primary purpose of adjectives can be either descriptive (*The shoe is shiny*) or limiting, restricting the noun's meaning, as in a statement like *Red shoes are on sale*, where the adjective *red* excludes non-red shoes.

Morphologically, most adjectives can be compared. The unmarked form of an adjective, such as *tall*, is its POSITIVE DEGREE. The COMPARATIVE degree, indicated by the inflectional morpheme *-er*, is used when comparing one thing to another (*taller*). The SUPERLATIVE degree, with *-est*, picks out one among several items as characterized by a quality to the highest degree (*tallest*). Comparative and superlative forms also apply to newly invented adjectives (*truthier, truthiest*). Some adjectives do not add the *-er* or *-est* morphemes, but instead use *more* and *most* (*more dangerous, most dangerous*). Some adjectives indicating absolute states, like *dead*, cannot be compared (**more dead, *most dead*).

Derivational morphemes that often occur in adjectives include *-able/-ible, -al, -ant/-ent, -ful, -ic, -ive, -ous*, and *-y* (*edible, adjectival, apparent, joyful, angelic, restive, raucous, tasty*), though words that contain – or appear to contain – these suffixes can also belong to other classes (*denial, arrive*, and so on), so this is not an infallible guide. Moreover, not all adjectives have such morphemes. When they do, however, they can provide interesting information about words. For instance, practically all adjectives ending in *-ous* were borrowed from French or Latin (*joyous, dangerous, prosperous*), whereas those ending in *-y* are predominantly of Anglo-Saxon origin (*mighty, thirsty, stony*).

Syntactically, adjectives can occur in three positions: an ATTRIBUTIVE adjective occurs before the structure it modifies (*the tall tree*); a POST-POSITIVE adjective occurs after it (*I consider the tree tall*); and a PREDICATIVE (or PREDICATE) adjective occurs after a linking verb (*The tree seems tall*). Some adjectives, many beginning with *a-*, cannot be used in *attributive* position: *abreast, afloat, afraid, alive, alone, awake*, and so on. One can say *The teenager is afraid/awake/alive/alone, The boat is afloat/abreast*, but not **The alone teenager* or **The afloat boat*. (Some of these adjectives do have related attributive forms that express similar meanings: *alive–living, alone–lone*.) A few other adjectives, like *main* or *former*, can only occur in the *attributive* position (**My reason is main, *I consider the reason main*). Finally, adjectives that accompany and modify pronouns are put in *post-positive* position: *something scary* (not **scary something*), *everyone present* (not **present everyone*). Adjectives can be stacked and rearranged: *the white new* *shoes, the new white shoes*. Finally, adjectives can be modified by *adverbs*: *very tall, almost dead, terribly dirty.*

Just as there are structures that are not nouns but behave like nouns (*nominals*), there are also words, phrases, and clauses that are not adjectives but function like them. Participles – the *-ing* and *-ed* forms of verbs – can often act like adjectives: *flying squirrels, dried herbs*. Phrases and clauses can also act like adjectives; in *the man from Portland* and *the horse which she rides, from Portland* and *which she rides* serve as modifiers that provide information about *the man* and *the horse*. Such structures are ADJECTIVALS.

Determiners

The primary function of DETERMINERS is to signal nouns, providing information about their definiteness, owner, location, or quantity. They include articles (*a, an, the*), possessive forms of nouns and pronouns (*my, her, Charlie's*), demonstratives (*this, these, that, those*), indefinites (*some, any, no, every*), and numbers (*one, two ...*). These words are traditionally classified as adjectives. However, determiners lack many of the features that characterize adjectives: they cannot be compared (**more the, *most an*); they cannot be stacked or rearranged (**a the an players, *an a the players*); and they cannot be modified by adverbs (**very the, *extremely an*). Also, when there are both a determiner and one or more adjectives modifying a noun, the determiner always comes first: *the dirty brown shoe* (not **dirty brown the shoe*).

As noted in the previous chapter, many nouns must be preceded by a determiner. **Dog barked* is not a legitimate sentence, whereas *The dog barked* is. The reason we identify articles, possessives, demonstratives, indefinites, and numbers as *determiners* is because they can all fulfill this function: *A dog barked, Her dog barked, That dog barked, Every dog barked*, and *One dog barked*.

29

A note on usage

Redundant adjectives name a quality already inherent in the noun they modify, like *advance warning* (any "warning" must come "in advance"), *final ultimatum* ("ultimatum" means "final conditions"), *foreign imports* (by definition, all "imports" are "foreign"), *free gift*, *old adage*, and *trite cliché*. When an adjective is redundant, it usually makes sense to cut it, unless you are aiming for a rhetorical effect, as Shakespeare does in *Hamlet*: "I will be brief: your noble son is mad: / Mad call I it; for, to define true madness, / What is't but to be nothing else but mad?"

Terms, Questions, and Exercises

ADJECTIVE, COMPARATIVE DEGREE, SUPERLATIVE DEGREE, ATTRIBUTIVE ADJECTIVE, POST-POSITIVE ADJECTIVE, PREDICATIVE (PREDICATE) ADJECTIVE, ADJECTIVAL, DETERMINER.

1. Name the semantic, morphological, and syntactic properties of adjectives.

2. Identify each of the underlined adjectives as attributive, post-positive, or predicative.

   a) Pizza is <u>delicious</u>.

   b) The <u>last</u> runner seems <u>slow</u>.

   c) The <u>kind</u> words only made him <u>angry</u>.

   d) There are two rooms <u>available</u>.

3. List the comparative and superlative forms for the following adjectives: *happy*; *fruitful*; *barbaric*; *few*; *generous*; *fine*; and *foolish*.

4. List five determiners that can replace *the* in *The victorious super-hero(es) returned*.

5. Name three different kinds of words that can function as determiners. Traditional grammars classify these as adjectives. Name two reasons why it makes better sense to assign these to a separate word class.

6. In the excerpt from Bulwer-Lytton's *Paul Clifford*, identify the adjectives and determiners: *It was a dark and stormy night; the rain fell in torrents—except at occasional intervals, when it was checked by a violent gust of wind which swept up the streets (for it is in London that our scene lies), rattling along the housetops, and fiercely agitating the scanty flame of the lamps that struggled against the darkness.*

7. Make up three phrases with redundant adjectives.

5. Verbs

As noted earlier, traditional definitions of the class of *verbs*, such as *The verb of a sentence expresses its action* or *Verbs denote actions, states of beings, or events*, are inadequate. In the first place, they are incomplete; in *I own a car*, the verb *own* does not describe an action, state of being, or an event; it indicates possession. Moreover, as with the other word classes, an accurate description of verbs must incorporate morphological and syntactic information. Finally, making generalizations about verbs is complicated by the fact that there are different kinds, with different semantic, morphological, and syntactic properties.

Let's begin by looking at the two broadest verb categories, for the distinction between them is fundamental: *main* (or *lexical*) *verbs* and *helping* (or *auxiliary*) *verbs*. Every sentence must have at least one main verb; helping verbs are optional and always accompany main verbs. There are also *primary verbs* – just three: *be, have*, and *do* – which can act either as main verbs (*I have a car*) or as helping verbs (*I have finished my chores*). In all, there are twelve helping verbs: the three primaries and nine *modal* verbs, which are *can, could, may, might, must, shall, should, will*, and *would*. Every verb other than these twelve is a main verb. (There are also a few verbs, the *semi-modals*, that have some but not all properties of modals; the most common ones are *dare, need, ought to*, and *used to*.) The chart below illustrates the relationship between main, helping, and primary verbs:

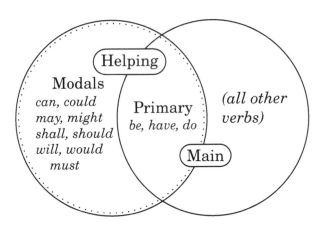

You should memorize the modal and primary verbs, including the different forms of *be*: *am, is, are; was, were; be, being, been.* There are some mnemonic tricks that you may find helpful here; for instance, the nine modals come in four pairs that begin with the same sound (*can / could, may / might, shall / should, will / would*) plus an "extra" (*must*). Of the eight forms of *be*, the three present-tense forms start with a vowel (*am, is, are*), the two past forms with a "w" (*was, were*), and the non-finite forms with a "b" (*be, being, been*). It may take you a bit of practice to memorize these, but you'll find the effort worth it.

Semantically, *main* verbs bear the primary meaning in a verb phrase while *helping* verbs complete or qualify that meaning. For example, in the sentence *Thomas might win,* the main verb is *win,* the helping verb *might.* In addition to actions, states, and events, verbs also typically express ownership (*The sword belongs to him*), cognitive processes or desires (*She knows it*), and measurement (*The statue weighs three tons*). Modal verbs convey information about the ability, likelihood, or necessity of the verb they accompany. For example, in *must remain, must* signifies that it is necessary to *remain.*

Main and modal verbs differ in morphology. Some main verbs have derivational suffixes like *-ate, -(i)fy,* and *-ise / -ize* (*advocate, verify, pulverize*), whereas modal verbs do not. The most important difference in morphology is that main verbs have four inflectional forms that differ from the verb's base form: present tense third person singular -s (shows); present participle -ing (showing); past tense -ed (showed); and past participle -n/-ed (shown). (*Base forms* and *participles* are discussed below, *tenses* in chapter 13.) Some main verbs do not follow this morphological pattern; they are IRREGULAR. This includes verbs that alternate the stem vowel, like *throw*: *she throws, she is throwing, she threw, she has thrown*. Other words, such as *burst*, omit the -n/-ed morphemes in the past and past participle forms: *The balloon bursts, the balloon is bursting, the balloon burst, the balloon has burst*. *Be* and *go* have entirely different forms in one or more contexts (*is, being, was/were, been; goes, going, went, gone*). However, all main verbs, as well as the primary verbs, have present tense third person singular -s and present participle -ing. Modal verbs have neither. Hence, forms like **coulds, *coulding, *mights*, or **mighting*, do not occur.

Main and modal verbs also have different syntactic properties. Main verbs can be turned into commands: *Drink it! Find him! Stop!* (Verbs expressing cognitive processes only rarely serve as commands, usually in set phrases like *Know this* or *Dream big*.) Modal verbs can never become commands (**Could! *May!*). When being negated, main verbs add a form of *do + not* before: *I care* turns into *I do not care, Charles lost* into *Charles did not lose*, and so on. Helping verbs omit the *do* and place the *not* after: *He is conceding* becomes *He is not conceding*. Most helping and primary verbs can also be contracted when negated: *can't, couldn't, mustn't, won't, wouldn't, shouldn't, isn't, haven't*, and *don't*. Another syntactic difference between main and helping verbs is that main verbs stay in place in questions and add *do* at the beginning of the sentence. Thus, *The whale surfaced* becomes *Did the whale surface?* However, if a helping verb is present, it is moved to the beginning and no form of *do* is added. Thus, *The whale might surface* becomes *Might the whale surface?* and *Madison will continue* becomes *Will Madison continue?*

Combining the preceding, we can conclude that the class of VERBS consists of main and helping verbs. MAIN verbs express actions, states, events, ownership, cognitive processes or desires, and measurement. Some main verbs have derivational morphemes, and all of them take inflectional morphemes (minimally, present tense third person singular-*s* and present participle *-ing*). Main verbs can be turned into commands, add *do* in questions, and add initial *do* + *not* when being negated. HELPING verbs complete or qualify main verbs, which they always accompany. MODAL verbs express ability, likelihood, or necessity. They do not have derivational morphemes and do not take *-s* or *-ing*. Modal verbs are not used as commands, are moved to initial position in yes-no questions, and, when being negated, do not add *do* and place the *not* after. The PRIMARY verbs *be*, *have*, and *do* can function as either main or helping verbs, and have some of the properties of each.

Participles and Infinitives

Main verbs have three special forms: the *-ing* form (PRESENT PARTICIPLE), the *-n* / *-ed* form (PAST PARTICIPLE), and the unmarked form that is often preceded by *to* (INFINITIVE).

The term "participle" comes from Latin *participium* – which means *participating* or *sharing* – because they share in features of several word classes. Present participles are used in *progressive* constructions like *I was flying* and *She will be flying*. They can be used with adjective function (*a flying bird*) or with noun function (*Flying is fun*). Past participles are used in *perfect* constructions such as *He has grown* and *He had grown*, as well as in *passive* constructions like *Tomatoes can be grown in greenhouses*. They can also be used with adjective function (*a grown lion*).

Infinitives come in two forms, the *to-infinitive* (*to leave*) and the *bare infinitive* (*leave*). To-infinitives often function nominally or adverbially. In *To leave might violate our agreement*, *to leave* acts as a nominal, as becomes evident through substitution (*It might violate our agreement*). In *To leave, you must first open the door, to leave* acts like an adverb. (We will discuss adverbs and adverbials in the next chapter.) Many verbs also take to-infinitive complements: *want to know, learn to fly, hope to hear, love to see, hate to discover*, and so on. *Bare infinitives* constitute the base form of a verb. They are generally used with *do* in questions and emphatic statements; for instance, *The train leaves soon* becomes and *The train does leave soon* and *Does the train leave soon?*

A note on usage

In chapter 3, we discussed *nominalization*, the process of turning words of a different class into nouns. The equivalent process for verbs, VERBIFICATION or VERBING, can also be problematic. Like nominalization, verbing is a normal language process, creating useful and unremarkable new verbs like *to drink, to merge*, and *to stop*, to say nothing of *to blog, to friend someone*, and *to google something*. Yet, clunky words like *actioning, dialoging*, or *efforting* can bog down writing. Business jargon is especially fond of verbing, creating terms like *commoditize, componentize, incentivize, monetize, securitize*, and others. Like all jargon, these words allow insiders to communicate quickly and efficiently. Outside of a business setting, however, terms like *commoditize* and *securitize* will probably raise red flags and are therefore best avoided.

Terms, Questions, and Exercises

VERB, MAIN (LEXICAL) VERB, HELPING (AUXILIARY) VERB, MODAL VERB, PRIMARY VERB, IRREGULAR VERB, PRESENT PARTICIPLE, PAST PARTICIPLE, INFINITIVE, VERBIFICATION (VERBING).

1. List the semantic, morphological, and syntactic properties of *main* and *modal* verbs.

2. List the bare infinitive and to-infinitive of the following verb forms: *shopping*, *smiles*, and *shown*.

3. In the passage below (another famous opening sentence), identify each underlined word in the following passage as a main, primary, or modal verb. For each primary verb, further specify whether it is acting like main verb (*I am hungry* or *I have chicken pox*) or a helping verb (*I am going* or *I have decided*).

   No one would have believed in the last years of the nineteenth century that this world was being watched keenly and closely by intelligences greater than man's and yet as mortal as his own; that as men busied themselves about their various concerns they were scrutinised and studied, perhaps almost as narrowly as a man with a microscope might scrutinise the transient creatures that swarm and multiply in a drop of water. – H. G. Wells, The War of the Worlds (1897)

4. Revise the expressions below by substituting more common expressions for the underlined instances of verbing:

   a) They greenlighted the proposal.

   b) Then, we actioned its ideas.

   c) Finally, we solutioned the problems that arose.

6. Adverbs and Prepositions

ADVERBS are extremely versatile, being able to modify verbs (*She went quietly*), other adverbs (*She went relatively quietly*), adjectives (*She is relatively tall*), and even whole sentences (*Fortunately, there is no rain in the forecast*).

Semantically, adverbs express a wide range of meanings and answer specific questions. The most frequently occurring adverbs refer to PLACE / MOTION, such as *here, inside, backward* (answering the question *Where?*); TIME, like *now, earlier, later* (*When?*); DURATION / FREQUENCY, such as *temporarily, always, often* (*How long? / How often?*); MEASURE/DEGREE, like *very, somewhat, entirely* (*To what extent?*); MANNER, such as *loudly, seriously, expertly* (*How?*); MODALITY, like *maybe, perhaps, probably* (*How certain?*); POINT OF VIEW, such as *personally, undoubtedly, undeniably*; and FOCUS, like *also, enough, only, too. Adverbs of measure / degree* are also called INTENSIFIERS. Focus adverbs call attention to a particular sentence element, especially by addition (*additionally, as well, even, too*), limitation (*exactly, exclusively, just, merely, purely, simply, solely*), and partial limitation (*chiefly, especially, mostly, particularly, primarily*). Intensifiers and focus adverbs are among the most commonly occurring modifiers in English.

In morphology, some adverbs – those of duration / frequency, measure/degree, and manner – have comparative and superlative degrees, but these are only rarely indicated by inflectional morphemes. The exceptions are forms that are identical to adjectives, such as *harder*: adverbial *work harder* and *work hardest* are analogous to adjectival *the harder / hardest stone*. Many adverbs of manner have derivational suffixes that give clues as their nature, *-wise* and *-ly* (*otherwise, likewise, hap-*

pily, quietly). Some adjectives can also end in *-ly*, especially when the suffix means "like an *x*," as in *beastly* (like a beast), *cowardly* (like a *coward*), and so on (*kingly, manly, princely, queenly, womanly*). Still, the vast majority of words ending in *-ly* are adverbs. The suffix *-ward(s)* often indicates an *adverb of place / motion* (*homeward, toward, forward, backward, upward, downward*).

Syntactically, adverbs' distinguishing feature is that they are mobile. For example, in the three-word sentence *She went quietly*, the adverb *quietly* can occur as the first, second, or third word: *Quietly she went, She quietly went, She went quietly*. When they modify adjectives or other adverbs, however, adverbs display less mobility, always coming before the word they modify. Despite this caveat, adverbs are the most mobile words in English.

The CONJUNCTIVE ADVERB is a special kind of adverb that links clauses; unlike true conjunctions, conjunctive adverbs form only a *semantic* link between clauses, not a *syntactic* one. This is apparent from two facts: conjunctive adverbs can always be removed without disturbing a sentence, and they can be moved within the clause to which they belong. For instance, in *She heard the explosion. However, she continued walking*, *however* is a transitional statement pointing back to *She heard the explosion*. It can be removed: *She heard the explosion. She continued walking*. It can be moved to any one of three positions in the clause: the beginning (*However, she heard the explosion*), after the subject (*She, however, heard the explosion*), and the end (*She head the explosion, however*). Common conjunctive adverbs include *also, however, instead, likewise, moreover, nevertheless, still, therefore*, and *thus*. They can be individual words or several that act as a single unit, such as *by contrast, in fact, in comparison*, and *on the other hand*.

By analogy with *nominal* and *adjectival*, the term ADVERBIAL refers to a structure that is not an adverb but acts like one. In addition to the usual meanings expressed by adverbs – place

/ motion, time, frequency / duration, and so on – adverbials often convey more complex information, including cause-effect relationships, as in *I went there because of the note*.

Prepositions

The word PREPOSITION gives a clue about its nature: it is a word "positioned before (pre-)" its complement, the OBJECT OF THE PREPOSITION, together with which it forms a PREPOSITIONAL PHRASE. Prepositions commonly express relations of *space* (*in, on, over*), *time* (*before, after*), and *logic* (*of, for, due to*). Prepositional phrases function as adverbials or adjectivals. When they modify nouns, as in *The house on the hill*, prepositional phrases are adjectival; *on the hill* gives us more information about the house. When they modify verbs, as in *She slept on the hill*, they function adverbially: here *on the hill* functions like an adverb of place, telling us where the sleeping took place.

The most common prepositions are *at, by, in, of, on, over, to*, and *up*. One-word prepositions are *simple*, while ones having two or more words are *complex*; examples of the latter include *because of, due to, instead of, out of, in addition to, in spite of*, and *on account of*. Words like *addition, spite*, and *account* may look like nouns, but they do not act as such; they cannot be pluralized or preceded by a determiner (**in an addition to*, **in the spite of*, **on accounts of*). In each case, the entire group of words has become frozen into a fixed expression that acts like a single word.

In the vast majority of cases, the *object of the preposition* is a noun or nominal: *at night, by the lake, of her, on the mountain, to Bob*. Sometimes, the object of a preposition will be another prepositional phrase, as in *from under the bed* or *until after dinner*. Occasionally, adverbs function as objects: *until recently, from here, to there, like now*. In a few rare cases, the object of the preposition will be an adjective, as in *The*

41

assassins left them for dead.

Prepositional phrases form tight bonds. Much as a determiner signals the presence of a noun, a preposition points ahead to its object. However, in certain situations, preposition and object can be separated, in which case the preposition is STRANDED. This often happens in questions (*What did you learn about?*) and in relative clauses (*The man I bought the car from*).

How to distinguish adverbs, prepositions, and related words

Adverbs and prepositions are easy to confuse. Both also resemble VERB PARTICLES, words that have become attached to main verbs; together, the verb and verbal particle form a single PHRASAL VERB. Some words, like *up*, can play any of the three roles: in *The smoke went up*, *up* is an adverb of place / motion identifying where the smoke *went*; in *The smoke went up the chimney*, *up* is a preposition whose object is *the chimney*; and, in *The letter turned up*, *up* is a verbal particle that, together with *turned*, forms the phrasal verb *turn(ed) up*. With a bit of practice, you can learn to distinguish adverbs, prepositions, and verb particles.

The key feature of phrasal verbs is that they are IDIOMATIC, that is, their meaning cannot be determined by analyzing the meaning of each individual word. In the sample sentence cited above, *The letter turned up*, *turned up* has the idiomatic meaning "be discovered." This meaning is idiomatic because it is not simply a form of *turn* + adverb of place / motion, like *turned left*. The basic meaning of the verb *turn* is changed by the addition of the particle *up*. Also, phrasal verbs can almost always be rephrased as one-word (sometimes two-word) expressions. *Turn up*, for instance, is synonymous with "appear." *Give up* means "surrender," *make up* "invent," and *shut up* "cease talking." (*Turn left* does not have a one-word equivalent.)

With this information in mind, we can formulate a test that will determine whether a word is verbal particle, a preposition, or an adverb:

Step 1: Try removing the word in question. If this changes the basic meaning of the verb, identify a one-word synonym for the phrasal verb; if you can do so, the word is a *verb particle*, and you do not have to move on to steps 2 and 3.

Step 2: Look for the object of the preposition. A preposition and its object form a single unit that provides information similar to an adjective or an adverb. If this is the case here, the word is a *preposition*, and you do not have to move on to step 3.

Step 3: To confirm that the word is an *adverb*, consider what kind of meaning it provides and what word(s) it is modifying. (Most adverbs that can be easily confused with prepositions or verbal particles are adverbs of place / motion that modify verbs.)

Let us consider a few examples.

First, *Bob counts on help*:

Step 1: When we remove *on*, we are left with *Bob counts help*; "counting on" help is very different from "counting" help. *Counting on* something means the same thing as *expecting* it. *On* is a *verb particle*.

Next, *Bob sits on the bench*:

Step 1: When we remove *on*, we are left with *Bob sits the bench*; "sitting" and "sitting on" are not different activities. In this context, *to sit on* does not have an idiomatic meaning, nor are there obvious one-word synonyms for the expression. *On* is not a *verb particle*.

Step 2: Here *on* requires *the bench* to complete its meaning; *Bob sits on* is not a valid expression. *On the bench* forms a single unit that provides adverbial information; specifically, it resembles an adverb of place / motion that modifies *sit* (telling us where Bob is sitting). *On* is a *preposition*.

Now, *Bob played on*:

43

Step 1: When we remove *on*, we are left with *Bob played*; "playing" is quite similar to "playing on." As in the previous example, *to play on* does not have any special meaning; it simply denotes "continue playing." *On* cannot be a *verb particle*.

Step 2: *On* is not followed by any other words, and it does not look like not a stranded preposition, so it cannot be a preposition.

Step 3: *On* provides information about "playing." Specifically, it tells us about the *duration* of the activity. This confirms that *on* is an *adverb*.

Finally, a more challenging example: *Bob will stay here next Thanksgiving*.

Step 1: *To stay* and *to stay here* are identical activities; in both cases, *stay* means "remain." Since *here* does not fundamentally alter the meaning of *stay*, it cannot be a *verb particle*.

Step 2: If *here next Thanksgiving* were a prepositional phrase, *next Thanksgiving* (an adjective and a noun) would be the object of the preposition *here*. However, *here next Thanksgiving* does not function as a unit. It provides not one but two kinds of information, answering the questions *Where?* (*here*) and *When?* (*next Thanksgiving*). Therefore, *here* is not a preposition.

Step 3: *Here* is an adverb of place, telling us *where* Bob will stay (*here*). *Thanksgiving* is a noun that provides information about time; along with its modifier *next*, it functions as an adverbial of time, telling us *when* Bob will be staying here (*next Thanksgiving*).

As the last example shows, nouns naming times and places – *The doctor will see you Thursday* or *We are home* – often have adverbial meaning. We can think of such expressions as having implied prepositions: *The doctor will see you [on] Thursday* , *We are [at] home*. This is true for our example sentence as well: *Bob will stay here [during] next Thanksgiving*. This confirms the adverbial nature of *next Thanksgiving*.

Difficult cases such as in *Bob will stay here next Thanksgiving* are the exception. It is usually not hard to tell the difference between verb particles, prepositions, and adverbs.

However, even the knottiest constructions can be unraveled with patience and the three-step method described above.

In closing, let us consider a much simpler problem, namely distinguishing adverbs from identical adjectives. Doing so only requires remembering that adjectives usually modify nouns, while adverbs typically modify verbs. *Slow* is adverbial in *fly slow* (*fly* is a verb), but adjectival in *slow plane* (*plane* is a noun); *late* is adverbial in *work late*, but adjectival in *late bus*; and *straight* is adverbial in *walk straight* but adjectival in *straight road.*

A note on usage

This will be the first of several notes on punctuation. If your grasp of this subject is shaky, you may want to read chapter 27, which provides an overview of punctuation.

As noted above, conjunctive adverbs can be moved to either sentence-initial, post-subject, or sentence-final position. They do not form tight syntactic bonds with their surrounding structures. Because they are parenthetic elements, they are always marked off with commas: *Moreover, the tire began to wobble*; *The tire, moreover, began to wobble*; *The tire began to wobble, moreover.*

Terms, Questions, and Exercises

ADVERB, ADVERB OF PLACE / MOTION, ADVERB OF TIME, AD-VERB OF DURATION / FREQUENCY, ADVERB OF MEASURE / DEGREE (INTENSIFIER), ADVERB OF MANNER, MODAL AD-VERB, POINT OF VIEW ADVERB, FOCUS ADVERB, CONJUNC-TIVE ADVERB, ADVERBIAL, PREPOSITION, OBJECT OF THE PREPOSITION, PREPOSITIONAL PHRASE, STRANDED PREPO-SITION, VERB PARTICLE, PHRASAL VERB, IDIOM (IDIOMATIC EXPRESSION).

1. What are the semantic, morphological, and syntactic properties of adverbs?

2. Name five phrasal verbs and give a one-word synonym for each.

3. Identify the word or group of words modified by each of the underlined adverbs, then categorize the adverb by kind (place / motion, time, etc.).

   a) The mouse sniffed at the cheese <u>hungrily</u>.

   b) The cat crept <u>forward</u>.

   c) <u>Personally</u>, I did not like the performance.

   d) We had a <u>much</u> better team.

   e) The two facts are <u>only</u> <u>tangentially</u> related.

4. What is the "object of a preposition"? Given an example. What is a "stranded preposition"? Give an example.

5. In the following sentences, identify the underlined words as adverbs or adjectives.

   a) The <u>friendly</u> gorilla followed her <u>gladly</u>.

   b) Saudi Arabia's <u>yearly</u> rainfall falls <u>almost</u> <u>daily</u> in Oregon's <u>rainy</u> season.

   c) This is <u>just</u> enough information to reach a <u>just</u> decision.

6. In the following sentences, identify the underlined words as adverbs, verbal particles, or prepositions. (Remember that in some expressions – such as *inside out* or *in order to* – the whole phrase counts as a single adverb or preposition.)

   a) <u>In</u> the morning we will carry <u>on</u> the fight.

   b) The concert was delayed <u>due</u> <u>to</u> the storm.

   c) Delighted <u>by</u> all the fans who showed <u>up</u> <u>for</u> the performance, the band played <u>with</u> great energy.

   d) You can put me <u>down</u>, but I won't stay <u>there</u>.

7. Punctuate the conjunctive adverbs in the sentences below:

   a) In addition many cooks value heirloom vegetables for their rich flavors.

   b) Hybrids have the advantage of being easier to care for however.

   c) Heirloom vegetables moreover vary more in size and appearance than hybrids.

7. Pronouns

PRO-NOUN means "for a noun," indicating the pronoun's most important function: to stand in for nouns and noun phrases. This property can be used to identify both pronouns and noun phrases. For example, *The cat jumped over the fence* can become *It jumped over the fence* or *The cat jumped over it*, a clue that both *the cat* and *the fence* are noun phrases. There are several different sub-classes of pronouns, including *personal, reflexive, reciprocal, relative, interrogative, demonstrative*, and *indefinite* pronouns. Each type of pronoun plays a different role within a sentence.

Personal pronouns

PERSONAL PRONOUNS are used for self-reference ("I," "me"), to address a listener ("you"), or to refer to an ANTECEDENT that has already been referenced ("he," "she," "it"). Occasionally, they can also look ahead to a later expression (technically, a postcedent), as in *While she waited, Sherry read a book*; "it" can also serve as subject place-holder (*It is raining*). Personal pronouns agree with the antecedent in number (singular or plural) and person (first, second, or third).

Personal pronouns have a *subject, possessive*, and *object* form. In *Bob's car hit a tree*, *Bob's* is possessive, *Bob's car* a subject, and *a tree* an object. For personal pronouns, the *subject* forms are, in the singular, *I* (first person), *you* (second person), and *he, she, it* (third person); in the plural, they are *we* (first person), *you* (second person), and *they* (third person). The *possessive* forms are, in the singular, *my / mine* (first person), *your / yours* (second person), and *his, her / hers*, and *its*; in the plural, they are *our / ours* (first person), *your / yours* (second person), and *their / theirs* (third person). The object forms are, in the singular, *me* (first person), *you* (second person), and *him, her*, and *it*; in the plural, they are *us* (first person), *you* (second person), and *them* (third person).

You may notice some patterns in the above list. For example, an -*s* ending indicates a possessive form (*his, hers, its, theirs*), while an -*m* ending signals an object form (*him, them*). This is one of the last remnants of the Old English *case* system, which signaled grammatical relationships through inflectional endings. Every noun and adjective had such endings, and the Old English adjective endings run parallel to the modern English pronoun endings. For instance, *heard stan* was the subject form of "hard stone," *heardes stanes* the possessive form, and *heardum stane* one of the object forms (the *dative*). This elaborate system has largely disappeared in modern English. We no longer mark the object forms of nouns with inflectional endings; whereas Old English had hundreds of inflectional endings, modern English has just eight.

Reflexive, Reciprocal, Demonstrative, and Indefinite pronouns

REFLEXIVE pronouns, which always end in -*self* or -*selves* – *myself, oneself, ourselves*, and so on – most often occur when the subject of a sentence is named again in the object. For example, we say *John kicked himself*, not *John kicked John*. Reflexive pronouns are also used for emphasis, as in *The President himself made the announcement*, which stresses that the announcement was made by the President personally, not by anyone else (such as the White House Press Secretary).

The RECIPROCAL pronouns *each other* and *one another* indicate mutual relationships, as in *The antagonists faced one another.*

DEMONSTRATIVE pronouns (*this, these, that, those*) indicate location, with *this* (plural *these*) referring to something close and *that* (plural *those*) to something distant. The relationship expressed can be one of space, time, or logic: *This is the Earth* versus *That is the moon*; *This is now* versus *That was then*; and *This is good* and *That is bad*. When used before a noun, as in *Those trips were educational* or *This sword is ancient*, demonstrative pronouns function as determiners.

INDEFINITE pronouns are "not definite"; they do not reference a specific being, location, and so on. Indefinite pronouns are commonly distributive (*each, every*), existential/universal (*all, any, some*), or indicative of degree (*few, less, little, more, most*). Like demonstratives, indefinite pronouns often function as determiners.

To distinguish pronouns from determiners, remember that pronouns "stand for" nouns while determiners provide more information about them. In *Some people like ice-cream*, *some* is a determiner because it modifies *people*; in *Some like ice-cream*, *some* is an indefinite pronoun.

Relative pronouns

A RELATIVE PRONOUN (*who / whose / whom, which, that*) heads a relative clause, an adjectival that modifies a preceding noun or nominal. Relative pronouns can often be omitted, as in *the pizza [which] I love*.

Like the personal pronouns, the relative *who* – which normally refers to people – has three forms; *who* is subjective, *whose* possessive, and *whom* objective. Just as native speakers are often confused as to when to use *I* or *me* and *he* or *him*, they can have difficulty deciding whether *who* or *whom* is correct.

Which is generally used to refer to objects, abstractions, and other non-personal nouns or nominals. It can also refer to entire clauses, as in *The grandstand collapsed, which was a tragedy.*

The relative pronoun *that*, which is generally regarded as more informal than *who* and *which*, can be used both personally and non-personally.

For more on relative clauses, see chapter 23.

Interrogative pronouns

INTERROGATIVE pronouns are used when "interrogating," that is, asking questions. They are *who, whom, whose, what*, and *which*. Except for *what / that*, this list exactly coincides with the relative pronouns, to which the interrogative pronouns are very similar. Likewise, when used to form questions, *where, when, how*, and *why* are often considered *interrogative adverbs*. Together, interrogative pronouns and adverbs form the class of INTERROGATIVES, or *wh-question words*.

The difference between interrogative and relative pronouns concerns function. As already mentioned, relative pronouns stand at the beginning of relative clauses, which are *adjectival*. Interrogative pronouns are used to ask *wh-questions*. These questions can also be embedded within other clauses, in which case they are usually *nominals*. For example, *Which horse won?* can become *I know which horse won*, which is functionally analogous to *I know it* or *I know Seabiscuit*. Thus, *which horse won* is an *interrogative clause*.

For more on interrogative clauses, see chapter 20.

Table 7.1 details the different kinds of pronouns and their members.

A note on usage

As noted above, modern English has abandoned subject and object forms, and this collapse has affected the pronoun system

	Function	Members
Personal	Refers to a noun / nominal (antecedent)	
Subject	Used in subject case (*I see the cat*)	*I, you, he, she, it; we, you, they*
Object	Used in object case (*Ally sees me*)	*Me, you, him, her, it; us, you, them*
Possessive, attributive	Used before noun (*Her cat slept*)	*My, your, his, her, its; our, your, their*
Possessive, predicative	Used after linking verb (*It is mine*)	*Mine, yours, his, hers, its; ours, yours, theirs*
Reflexive	Used when object pronoun refers to subject	*Myself, yourself, himself, herself, itself; ourselves, yourselves, themselves*
Reciprocal	Indicates mutual relationships	*Each other, one another*
Demonstrative	Indicates "distance" (in location, time, logic)	*This, these, that, those*
Indefinite	Refers to non-specific beings, objects, etc.	*All, another, any, anyone, anything, both, each, either, enough, every, everyone, everything, few, fewer, less, many, more, most, much, none, plenty, quite a few, several, some, someone, something, what(ever)*
Relative	Heads relative clause	*Who, whose, whom, which, that*
Interrogative	Forms questions	*Who, whose, whom, which, what*

Table 7.1.: Pronouns

as well. Even native speakers of English often find themselves wondering whether to use *I* or *me*, *he* or *him*, and *she* or *her.*

The difficulty is especially pronounced in paired pronouns, as in *I and he are good friends.* In some varieties of English, this would become *Me and him are good friends.* (The influence of *paired* pronouns can be observed in the fact that, when we delete one, the resulting sentence sounds obviously wrong: **Me am his good friend, *Him is my good friend*).

Because of the stigma associated with expressions like *Me and him are good friends*, we often *hyper-correct* in formal situations, using a proper-sounding but incorrect form in place of the less proper-sounding but actually correct one. For instance, **Charles waved at Daniel and I* should be *Charles waved at Daniel and me*, as becomes apparent when we drop the *Daniel and*; that is, **Charles waved at I* is incorrect and *Charles waved at me* correct.

Therefore, if you are confused by paired pronouns, or a pronoun joined to a noun phrase or nominal, try deleting the other element.

Terms, Questions, and Exercises

PRONOUN, PERSONAL PRONOUN, ANTECEDENT, REFLEXIVE PRONOUN, RECIPROCAL PRONOUN, DEMONSTRATIVE PRONOUN, INDEFINITE PRONOUN, RELATIVE PRONOUN, INTERROGATIVE PRONOUN, INTERROGATIVE.

1. Name five personal pronouns, five reflexive pronouns, five indefinite pronouns, and one reciprocal pronoun.

2. Name the relative pronouns. How does this list differ from the interrogative pronouns? In addition to pronouns, what other kinds of words are interrogatives?

3. In the following sentences, identify the kind of pronoun that each underlined word represents:

a) I already know <u>that</u>.

b) The class <u>which</u> met early challenged <u>them</u>.

c) <u>Who</u> did this?

d) They recognized <u>each other</u>.

e) Michael did the most difficult problems <u>himself</u>; <u>these</u> stumped many <u>others</u>.

4. In the sentences below, identify the underlined words as pronouns or determiners:

a) <u>That</u> store carries <u>none</u>.

b) <u>That</u> is <u>our</u> tree house.

c) <u>Some</u> find heights disturbing.

5. Indicate the formal form of the underlined pronouns below; if no change is required, write "correct."

a) <u>Me and him</u> saw the squirrel climb the feeder.

b) The waiter asked <u>her and I</u> what we wanted to drink.

c) I watched <u>she and he</u> play a duet.

8. Conjunctions and Interjections

CONJUNCTIONS link together – "con-join" – grammatical units, allowing for the creation of far more sophisticated sentences than would otherwise be the case. The two main types are COORDINATING CONJUNCTIONS, which link words, phrases, or clauses and give them equal semantic weight, and SUBORDINATING CONJUNCTIONS (or simply SUBORDINATORS), which link only clauses and make one less important than ("subordinate" to) the other.

Coordinating conjunctions

There are seven coordinating conjunctions: *for*, *and*, *nor*, *but*, *or*, *yet*, and *so*. These words' initial letters form the acronym FANBOYS. In studying conjunctions, your first step should be to memorize these. Once you know them by heart, you will find it easy to distinguish coordinating and subordinating conjunctions: any conjunction that's *not* one of the FANBOYS must be a subordinating conjunction.

As already mentioned, coordinating conjunctions can join words (*Bob or Bill*), phrases (*up the hill and down the hill*), and clauses (*We played well, yet they won.*) The structures joined must be of similar kind, ruling out constructions like **Bob and down the hill*. Not all the FANBOYS can join each type of element. *And*, *but*, and *or* can, but the other four are more limited. *For*, *yet*, and *so* almost always join only clauses: (**Bob yet Bill*, **up the hill for down the hill*); the exception is that *yet* can join adjectives and adverbs (*thin yet strong, lightly yet firmly*). *Nor* only rarely occurs on its own, and, when it does, sounds somewhat formal, as in *The rain fell, nor did it stop*); *nor* is usually preceded by *not* or *neither*.

A sub-type of the coordinating conjunction, the CORRELATIVE CONJUNCTION, extends the coordinating conjunction by prefixing it with another expression, creating a balanced expression. The correlative conjunctions are *both ... and, whether ... or, either ... or, neither ... nor*, and *not only ... but also*.

When a coordinating conjunction joins two clauses, it gives them equal weight; therefore, the clauses are said to be *independent*. The traditional definition of an independent clause is that it "expresses a complete thought and can stand on its own." This is not wrong, but it *is* misleading. For example, in *He laughed but she frowned, but she frowned* is an independent clause, yet it cannot stand on its own and doesn't express a complete thought. If you omit the conjunction at the beginning, the clause will pass the test, but so would most subordinate clauses like *After we left*. A better definition is that INDEPENDENT CLAUSES are clauses not headed by a subordinating conjunction. This makes our job simple: *if a clause begins with one of the* FANBOYS, *it's independent; if a clause does not begin with a conjunction at all, it's also independent*. Problem solved!

Subordinating conjunctions

A DEPENDENT CLAUSE is headed by a subordinating conjunction and is embedded within an independent clause (its MATRIX CLAUSE). There are three types of dependent clauses, each headed by a different kind of subordinator: nominal dependent clauses begin with an interrogative or *that, if,* or *whether*; relative clauses function as adjectives and begin with a relative pronoun; and adverbial dependent clauses begin with an ADVERBIAL CONJUNCTION. Of the subordinators, you've already encountered interrogatives and relative pronouns in the previous chapter; only the adverbial conjunctions are new. Adverbial conjunctions include expressions such as *because, since, when, while, as soon as,* and *in order to.* To create an adverbial clause, simply attach an adverbial subordinator to the beginning of an independent clause: *He dances well* can become *Because he dances well. He dances well* is independent, but *Because he dances well* requires a matrix clause: *Because he dances well, he likes to Salsa.* In addition to the kinds of meanings often expressed by adverbs, such as time, place/motion, duration/frequency, and so on, adverbial clauses often provide more complex information, describing logical relationships such as causes, conditions, reasons, and purposes. (These predominantly answer the question *Why?*) Also, like adverbs, adverbial clauses are mobile; they can be moved either before or after their matrix clause: *Because he dances well, he likes to Salsa* / *He likes to Salsa because he dances well.*

To identify a nominal subordinate clause, look for the interrogative or *that, if,* or *whether* at its beginning; also, you will usually be able to substitute a pronoun (either personal, like *it,* or indefinite, such as *something*) for the whole clause. Relative clauses are headed by a relative pronoun (*who/whom/whose, which,* and *that*) and are adjectival, providing further information about the noun or nominal they follow. (In some cases, relative subordinators can be omitted: *The book I'm reading is a teen paranormal romance.* If you suspect this to be the case, try inserting one: *The book which I'm reading is a teen paranormal romance.*) Adverbial clauses begin with an adverbial subordinator; they can be moved before or after the matrix clause.

Adverbial conjunctions look very similar to prepositions. In fact, some words can function as either prepositions or subordinating conjunctions: *since* is a preposition in *since Tuesday* but a conjunction in *since the train left*; *until* is a preposition in *until midnight* but a conjunction in *until we meet again*; and so on. Many of the words that have this dual function create structures that indicate *time*; in addition to *since* and *until*, these include *after*, *before*, and *for*. Other prepositions that look like subordinating conjunctions will usually have an added particle, as in *because* (conjunction) versus *because of* (preposition) and *as* (conjunction) versus *as of* (preposition).

The difference between prepositions and subordinating conjunctions lies in their complements. Because prepositions take phrases as complements, they will lack the *subject + predicate* structure. By contrast, subordinating conjunctions will always follow the *subject + predicate* structure. This is only way to distinguish prepositions from subordinating conjunctions.

True to the similarity in their names, adverbial conjunctions are also similar to the conjunctive adverbs discussed in chapter 6. To keep them apart, remember that conjunctions form tight bonds with the clauses to which they're joined. Adverbial subordinators cannot be moved within their clauses. (The adverbial clause as a whole can be moved before or after the matrix clause, but the conjunction on its own cannot be moved.) *Because he dances well* cannot become **He, because, dances well*. A conjunctive adverb *can* be moved within the clause; *However, he dances well* could be rewritten *He, however, dances well* or *He dances well, however.*

Interjections

INTERJECTIONS are exclamatory utterances that most commonly express an emotional reaction (*oops*, *ouch*, *wow*) or describe a noise by imitating its sound (*bang*, *pow*, *wham*). They can also serve as conversational filler, as in *Hey, I want to go* or *He's, like, angry*. Other filler expressions are *well* and (increasingly) *so*, which have lost much of their adverbial force in conversation. They are rarely used in formal writing, except when reproducing dialogue.

Interjections should not be confused with *commands* such as *Stop!*, which have an implied *you* as agent (*You stop!*).

A note on usage

As described in chapter 6, conjunctive adverbs form only loose bonds with the clauses to which they belong; thus, they are marked off with commas. Conjunctions, however, form tight syntactic bonds with their complements. Therefore, no comma comes after the conjunction in a sentence like *Spencer played but, Dillon did not*. The exception is when there is an interrupting element set off with commas: *Spencer played but, to our surprise, Dillon did not*.

In formal written English, coordinating conjunctions cannot begin sentences. In more informal contexts, writers often do start sentences with *or*, *and*, or *but*, primarily to make sentences shorter. Writers also often place periods before a coordinating conjunction for rhetorical effect: *You could try again. Or you could walk away.* In such contexts, one could also use a dash: *You could try again — or you could walk away.* The latter sentence would be acceptable in formal written English. (For more on the dash, see chapter 27.)

When a coordinating conjunction joins two independent clauses, a comma goes before second: [clause], *and* [clause]. If the clauses are very short, the comma can be omitted: *Spencer played but Dillon did not*.

Subordinate clauses vary in how they are punctuated. Most often, nominals are not set off by punctuation. As we'll see in chapter 23, adjectival (relative) clauses are set off with commas when they are non-restrictive. Adverbial clauses take a comma when they come before the matrix clause (*Because he dances well, he likes to Salsa*) but only rarely after it (*He likes to Salsa because he dances well*). Concessive adverbial clauses – which "concede" a point that seems to contradict the matrix clause – are usually separated with a comma even when they come at the end of a sentence: *We considered it a bargain, although she thought otherwise*.

Terms, Questions, and Exercises

CONJUNCTION, COORDINATING CONJUNCTION, SUBORDINAT-
ING CONJUNCTION (SUBORDINATOR), FANBOYS, CORRELA-
TIVE CONJUNCTION, INDEPENDENT CLAUSE, DEPENDENT
(SUBORDINATE) CLAUSE, MATRIX CLAUSE, ADVERBIAL CON-
JUNCTION, INTERJECTION.

1. List the coordinating conjunctions as well as three correlative conjunctions.

2. What kinds of structures can coordinating conjunctions join? Which of them can join the full spectrum of structures, and which are more limited? For the ones that are more limited, what types of structures do they typically link?

3. How can you distinguish between coordinating conjunctions, subordinating conjunctions, and conjunctive adverbs?

4. Identify the underlined words or phrases as coordinating conjunctions, subordinating conjunctions, or conjunctive adverbs. (Their matrix clauses extend from the conjunction itself to the first following mark of punctuation.)

    a) <u>As</u> the antelope drank, the lion crept closer.

    b) Sarah exhaled <u>when</u> the results came in; <u>however,</u> she could not relax yet.

    c) Michael won, <u>yet</u> the team still lost.

    d) It never occurred to the sailors <u>that</u> pirates might be watching.

5. List the three types of subordinating conjunctions and the kinds of clauses they head. What are the identifying features of each kind of clause?

6. In the sentences below, identify the underlined subordinate clauses as nominal, relative, or adverbial.

   a) Everyone has heard <u>that elephants are afraid of mice</u>.

   b) <u>Although this seems like a myth</u>, the television program "Mythbusters" found some truth behind the idea.

   c) The elephant's musophobia, <u>which was first recorded by the Roman writer Pliny the Elder</u>, is actually mild.

   d) <u>What elephants fear even more</u> are ants, <u>who are able to get inside their trunks</u>.

7. How can you distinguish conjunctions from prepositions? Identify each of the underlined words below as a conjunction or preposition.

   a) <u>Since</u> the game was tied after regulation, it went into overtime.

   b) I haven't eaten <u>since</u> noon.

   c) The preparations <u>for</u> the party were extensive.

8. List five interjections.

9. Part 1 Review

Chapter 1 Terms
GRAMMAR, CLAUSE, PHRASE, PEDAGOGICAL GRAMMAR, PRE-SCRIPTIVE GRAMMAR, DESCRIPTIVE GRAMMAR, INFINITE USE OF FINITE MEANS, OLD ENGLISH, ORIGINS OF STANDARD LAN-GUAGE VARIETIES, KNOWLEDGE OF GRAMMAR, KNOWLEDGE ABOUT GRAMMAR, USAGE.

Chapter 2 Terms
WORD CLASS, SYNTAX, MORPHOLOGY, SEMANTICS, FUNC-TION SHIFT, FORM, FUNCTION, CONTENT WORDS, FUNCTION WORDS, OPEN WORD CLASSES, CLOSED WORD CLASSES, MOR-PHEME, ROOT MORPHEME, FREE MORPHEME, BOUND MOR-PHEME, AFFIX, PREFIX, SUFFIX, DERIVATIONAL MORPHEME, INFLECTIONAL MORPHEME.

Chapter 3 Terms
NOUN, PROPER NOUN, COMMON NOUN, COUNTABLE NOUN, UNCOUNTABLE NOUN, NOMINAL, NOMINALIZATION.

Chapter 4 Terms
ADJECTIVE, COMPARATIVE DEGREE, SUPERLATIVE DEGREE, ATTRIBUTIVE ADJECTIVE, POST-POSITIVE ADJECTIVE, PRED-ICATIVE (PREDICATE) ADJECTIVE, ADJECTIVAL, DETERMINER.

Chapter 5 Terms
VERB, MAIN (LEXICAL) VERB, HELPING (AUXILIARY) VERB, MODAL VERB, PRIMARY VERB, IRREGULAR VERB, PRESENT PARTICIPLE, PAST PARTICIPLE, INFINITIVE, VERBIFICATION

(VERBING).

Chapter 6 Terms
ADVERB, ADVERB OF PLACE / MOTION, ADVERB OF TIME, AD-
VERB OF DURATION / FREQUENCY, ADVERB OF MEASURE /
DEGREE (INTENSIFIER), ADVERB OF MANNER, MODAL AD-
VERB, POINT OF VIEW ADVERB, FOCUS ADVERB, CONJUNC-
TIVE ADVERB, ADVERBIAL, PREPOSITION, OBJECT OF THE
PREPOSITION, PREPOSITIONAL PHRASE, STRANDED PREPO-
SITION, VERB PARTICLE, PHRASAL VERB, IDIOM (IDIOMATIC
EXPRESSION).

Chapter 7 Terms
PRONOUN, PERSONAL PRONOUN, ANTECEDENT, REFLEXIVE
PRONOUN, RECIPROCAL PRONOUN, DEMONSTRATIVE PRO-
NOUN, INDEFINITE PRONOUN, RELATIVE PRONOUN, INTER-
ROGATIVE PRONOUN, INTERROGATIVE.

Chapter 8 Terms
CONJUNCTION, COORDINATING CONJUNCTION, SUBORDINAT-
ING CONJUNCTION (SUBORDINATOR), FANBOYS, CORRELA-
TIVE CONJUNCTION, INDEPENDENT CLAUSE, DEPENDENT
(SUBORDINATE) CLAUSE, MATRIX CLAUSE, ADVERBIAL CON-
JUNCTION, INTERJECTION.

0. (You should be able to recall the 8 inflectional morphemes,
   the 9 modal verbs, the 3 primary verbs, and the 7 coordinating conjunctions.)

1. What do we call the approach to studying grammar which
   teaches beginning students the rudiments of a formal, literary language? The approach that focuses on improving
   the student's language through a list of do's and don't's?
   The approach which takes an objective view to grammar,
   explaining how people actually use language, not how
   they ought to use it?

2. Shakespeare wrote his plays and poems around the year 1600. Would his works be considered "Old English"? Why or why not?

3. How does the standard variety of a language typically come about?

4. What is the difference between the open ("content") and closed ("function") word classes? Name four open and four closed classes.

5. What is an inflectional morpheme? How does it differ from a derivational morpheme? Name the eight inflectional morphemes.

6. List the individual morphemes comprising the following words. Describe each morpheme as either free or bound, then specify whether it is a root, a prefix, a derivational suffix, or an inflectional suffix:

   a) cupcake

   b) mileage's

   c) undoing

   d) inartful

7. How do traditional grammars define "parts of speech" such as nouns? What problems arise with this approach? On the basis of what three properties do descriptive grammars define word classes? Compare the traditional definition of the noun to our definition.

8. What are *nominalization* and *verbing*? What stylistic problems can they create? In what circumstances should they be avoided?

9. Name the three positions in which adjectives can occur. Give an example of each using the adjective *tall*.

10. Name the semantic, morphological, and syntactic properties of adjectives.

11. What do the words *any*, *her*, *five*, *Sebastian's*, *an*, and *these* have in common?

12. Fill in the blanks:

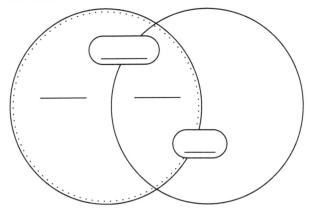

13. List the semantic, morphological, and syntactic properties of *main* and *modal* verbs.

14. Give the present participle, the past participle, the bare infinitive, and the to-infinitive of the verb *throw*.

15. Name the different kinds of pronouns and give an example of each. What is the primary purpose of each type of pronoun?

16. How can you distinguish the following kinds of words from one another:

   a) adverb (including conjunctive adverb)

   b) verb particle

   c) preposition

   d) conjunction

17. In the sentences below, identify the class of the underlined words:

   a) We did not slip <u>up</u> <u>on</u> the answer.

   b) We waited <u>until</u> the rain stopped.

   c) The tree fell <u>down</u> in the yard.

   d) You should check <u>out</u> the things <u>on</u> sale.

18. What word classes can adverbs modify? What are the major kinds of adverbs? To what question does each answer?

19. What is a "stranded preposition"? Give an example.

20. What are the coordinating conjunctions? What acronym is helpful for remembering them? What kinds of structures can they join? Which coordinating conjunctions join primarily clauses?

21. What are the three kinds of subordinating conjunctions and the kinds of clauses they head? What's the best way of identifying each?

22. Identify the underlined words or phrases as coordinating conjunctions, subordinating conjunctions, or conjunctive adverbs. (Their matrix clauses extend from the conjunction itself to the first following mark of punctuation.) For subordinating conjunctions, further identify the kind of clause they head (nominal, adjectival, or adverbial).

   a) <u>When</u> Thomas scored, the crowd cheered.

   b) <u>Therefore</u>, the problem has been solved.

   c) I like pizza, <u>so</u> I eat it often.

   d) The car, <u>which</u> had been speeding, slowed at the intersection.

   e) She wondered <u>where</u> her bike was.

23. To what class does the word *like* in the following expression belong? *She's, like, great at math.*

24. What are nominals, adjectivals, and adverbials? Give an example of each.

25. *(Challenge.)* The passage below opens Johnston McCulley's *The Curse of Capistrano* (1919), the first "Zorro" story. Using context to guide you, name the class of every word in the passage. (If a word occurs several times in the same function, you don't have to keep identifying it.) Be as precise as you can, specifying the particular subclass where possible (e.g., *primary* verbs, *coordinating* conjunctions, and so on). Categorize *-ing* and *-ed* forms that function as main verbs as "main verb"; if they do not function as main verbs, identify them as "present participle" or "past participle." (Do the best you can with the latter, but don't worry if it gives you difficulty, since we have not yet discussed participles in detail.) "'Tis" means "it is," and should treated as two words.

Again the sheet of rain beat against the roof of red Spanish tile, and the wind shrieked like a soul in torment, and smoke puffed from the big fireplace as the sparks were showered over the hard dirt floor.

"'Tis a night for evil deeds!" declared Sergeant Pedro Gonzales, stretching his great feet in their loose boots toward the roaring fire and grasping the hilt of his sword in one hand and a mug filled with thin wine in the other. "Devils howl in the wind, and demons are in the raindrops! 'Tis an evil night, indeed—eh, señor?"

Part II.

Phrases

10. Phrases and Phrase Structure

As we saw in the preceding section, language is modular. Every sentence can be broken down into clauses, every clause into phrases, and every phrase into words. Within this hierarchy, the phrase plays a crucial role. In this section, we will discuss the nature of phrases, the different kinds of phrases, and the various roles they play in a sentence.

At the outset, it is important to recognize an important difference in how traditional grammar and descriptive grammar define the *phrase*. Traditional grammar understands it, in the words of the *Merriam-Webster Dictionary*, as "a group of two or more words that express a single idea but do not usually form a complete sentence." The three kinds of phrases treated by traditional grammars are the prepositional phrase (*on the roof*), the infinitive phrase (*to fly*), and the gerund phrase (*cycling home*). Descriptive grammar assigns a much more prominent role to the phrase, defining it – as we did in chapter 1 – as a word or group of words functioning as a grammatical unit and not containing both subject and predicate. (Structures with subjects and predicates are *clauses*.) This definition superficially resembles the traditional one, but it differs in one key way, namely in that phrases can consist of individual words. As we will see, this distinction turns phrases from structures of secondary grammatical importance into the basic building-blocks – or CONSTITUENTS – of the sentence.

There are five kinds of phrases: the *noun phrase*, the *verb phrase*, the *adjective phrase*, the *adverb phrase*, and the *prepositional phrase*. Other than prepositional phrases – which, as we have already seen, are predominantly adjectival or adverbial in function – this list corresponds exactly to the four open word classes of *nouns*, *verbs*, *adjectives*, and *adverbs*.

Heads, Modifiers, and Complements

There is an intimate relationship between word class and phrase type. Every phrase has as its central element, or HEAD, a word that determines the nature of the phrase. Noun phrases are *headed* by a noun or pronoun, verb phrases by a verb, adjectives phrases by an adjective, adverb phrases by an adverb, and prepositional phrases by a preposition.

In addition, the five phrase types also share an underlying structure, which can be described as follows: (Pre-modifier) HEAD (Complement) (Post-Modifier).

MODIFIERS describe qualities or attributes of the head; PRE-MODIFIERS precede the head, while POST-MODIFIERS follow it. Modifiers are always *optional* and can be *stacked* – that is, several can occur in the same phrase – and modifiers of the same kind can be *rearranged* (though pre-modifiers cannot necessarily swap positions with post-modifiers). For instance, in the noun phrase *shiny new shoes with white laces in her closet*, the head *shoes* has two pre-modifiers, *shiny* and *new*, as well as two post-modifiers, *with white laces* and *in her closet*. Any or all of the four modifiers could be omitted: *shiny shoes in her closet*, *new shoes with white laces*, or simply *shoes*. We could also add a theoretically unlimited number of other modifiers *(shiny new white tennis shoes*, and so on). The order of pre-modifiers can be reversed *(shiny new shoes* or *new shiny shoes)*, and the same thing goes for the post-modifiers *(shoes with white laces in her closet* or *shoes in her closet with white laces)*.

Many phrases also admit or even require COMPLEMENTS, structures that complete the meaning of the head. Every prepositional phrase, for instance, requires a complement, as do certain kinds of verbs. Expressions such as **shoes in, *He threw,* and *I gave her* are incomplete because they lack required complements, prompting questions like "Shoes in *what*?", "*What* did he throw?", and "*What* did you give her?" Not all kinds of heads require complements. The sentence *Tracy drove* consists of a noun phrase (*Tracy*) and a verb phrase (*drove*) each containing only a head.

Some heads, like *call*, can take between zero and two complements: *Tristan called* has none; *Tristan called Tommy* has one (*Tommy*); and *Tristan called Tommy a genius* has two (*Tommy* and *a genius*). Therefore, we cannot define complements as being *required*, as traditional grammars do. Instead, because complements are present in some cases but not others, it is more accurate to say that particular heads allow or LICENSE complements. As head of a verb phrase, *call* licenses between zero and two complements. Modifiers are not licensed; they can be omitted, stacked, and rearranged, which is not the case with complements.

To illustrate this difference, let's return to the examples in the previous paragraph. Although *call* licenses between zero and two complements, the complements cannot be omitted or rearranged, nor can they be indefinitely stacked. Consider the verb phrase *called Tommy a genius*. If we *omit* the first complement, *Tommy*, we get *called a genius*, which is grammatically correct but fundamentally changes the meaning of the phrase, implying that you phoned someone like Stephen Hawking. Omitting *a genius* – resulting in *called Tommy* – also alters the basic meaning of *call*, because "calling someone" is not the same as "calling someone a genius." Nor can the order of the complements be *rearranged*; *called Tommy a genius* cannot become *called a genius Tommy*. Finally, we cannot *stack* more complements than allowed: *called Tommy Stephen a genius*. (*Tristan called Tommy and Stephen a genius* would require a conjunction.) The triple test of *omission*, *stacking*, and *rearrangement* allows us to distinguish between a complement licensed by a head and an optional modifier.

As a rule of thumb, the role of complement is most often

fulfilled by a nominal, while the role of modifier is most often played by an adjectival or adverbial. However, sometimes adjectivals and adverbials do function as complements. In sentences like *Tara is fast* or *Tony hails from the city*, the adjective *fast* and the adverbial *from the city* cannot be omitted (**Tara is*, **Tony hails*).

There are occasional exceptions to the (Pre-modifier) HEAD (Complement) (Post-Modifier) pattern. For instance, as we saw in chapter 6, constructions such as *What did you learn about?* feature a *stranded preposition*; *about*, which heads the prepositional phrase *about what*, is here separated from its complement *what*. In a sentence like *Pynchon I do not like*, the direct object *Pynchon* has been moved from its ordinary position for emphasis. In both cases, we could easily rearrange the "offending" structure to make it follow the standard pattern (*About what did you learn? I do not like Pynchon*). Departures from the normal phrase structure occur in a limited number of cases and for particular reasons; see chapter 26 for more details. Such exceptions should not obscure the fundamental importance of the (Pre-modifier) HEAD (Complement) (Post-Modifier) structure of phrases.

Nesting: phrases within phrases

Another important property of phrases is that, like Russian dolls, they can be nested inside one another. Nesting commonly occurs in verb and prepositional phrases, which often take noun phrase complements. To return to the examples above, the verb phrase *called Tommy a genius* consists of the head, *called*, and two noun phrase complements, *Tommy* and *a genius*. Likewise, the prepositional phrase *from the city* consists of the head *from* and the complement *the city*, also a noun phrase. Furthermore, prepositional phrases as a whole also often function as post-modifiers within noun phrases. For example, in *books on the third shelf from the top*, *books* is modified by the prepositional phrase *on the third shelf,* while *shelf* in turn is modified by *from the top.* Theoretically, there is no limit to the number of phrases that can be stacked inside one another.

Phrase structure trees

To represent these and other grammatical relationships, teaching grammars and descriptive grammars alike make use of visual diagrams. Teaching grammars typically use *Reed-Kellogg diagrams* such as the one below:

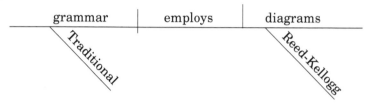

Descriptive grammars commonly employ PHRASE STRUCTURE TREES (also known as *PS trees* or just *trees*), which illustrate syntactic relationships through a system of *nodes* and *branches.* Although each method has its advantages, we will use Phrase Structure trees. The basic structure of phrases can be represented in the following tree:

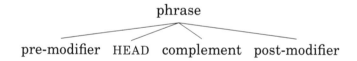

In the simplest trees, such as the one below, each *node* (*NP*, for *noun phrase*, and *N*, for *noun*) has only a single *branch*:

When representing syntactic structures, individual nouns – or adjectives, adverbs, and so on – are actually one-word phrases. Here, the noun phrase *shoes* consists only of a head and no modifiers or complements. A more complex phrase, *shiny new shoes*, features two pre-modifiers (adjectives) and a head (a noun), so this *NP* node has three branches:

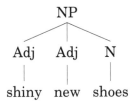

Finally, *shoes with white laces* illustrates how phrases can be stacked inside other phrases (*PP* stands for "prepositional phrase," *P* for "preposition"):

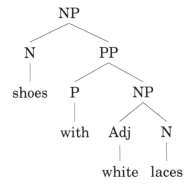

Phrase structure trees are useful for illustrating syntactic relationships.

A note on usage

Because phrases form a tightly organized unit, they usually do not have internal punctuation. In *little green, men from Mars*, *little green men, from Mars*, and *little green men from,*

Mars, commas disrupt the internal coherence of the phrase, coming between pre-modifier and head (**green, men*), head and post-modifier (**men, from Mars*), and head and complement (**from, Mars*), respectively. One of the few exceptions to this rule is the non-restrictive relative clause, a noun phrase post-modifier: *the little green men, who were from Mars*. Restrictive and non-restrictive relative clauses are discussed in chapter 23. When one or more intervening words do interrupt the internal structure of a phrase, it is set off with commas, parentheses, or dashes: *little green men from – where else? – Mars*.

Terms, Questions, and Exercises

PHRASE, CONSTITUENT, HEAD, MODIFIER, PRE-MODIFIER, POST-MODIFIER, COMPLEMENT, LICENSE, PHRASE STRUCTURE TREE.

1. What is the key difference in how traditional and descriptive grammar define the phrase? What role does the phrase play in descriptive grammar?

2. List the five basic kinds of phrases. For each, identify the class of the word that heads each.

3. What are the four different elements common to all types of phrases?

4. Explain the difference between complements and modifiers. What test can distinguish between them?

5. In the items below, brackets indicate phrase boundaries (not all phrase boundaries are marked). Words that appear in caps head the phrase in which they appear; complements are underlined and modifiers italicized. For each phrase, first specify its kind by identifying the class of the head, then identify the word class of each complement and modifier. *Example: [crafty MERCHANTS] = noun*

phrase; head = "merchant" (noun); pre-modifier = "crafty" (adjective)

   a) [BEARS] [HIBERNATE].

   b) [*Female* BEARS] HIBERNATE [DURING <u>winter</u>].

   c) [[*Quietly* CONFIDENT] INDIVIDUALS][*almost* ALWAYS] SUCCEED.

6. In *Female bears hibernate during, winter,* is the comma between "during" and "winter" correct? Why or why not?

11. Adjective, Adverb, and Prepositional Phrases

Adjective, adverb, and prepositional phrases serve primarily – though not exclusively – as modifiers, and they usually have a less complex structure than noun phrases and verb phrases. This makes it convenient to discuss adjective, adverb, and prepositional phrases together.

Adjective Phrases

ADJECTIVE PHRASES are headed by an adjective. The minimal adjective phrase is a single adjective, while more complex phrases can contain the full assortment of pre-modifiers, complements, and post-modifiers. Typically, adjective pre-modifiers consist of single adverbs, complements and post-modifiers of phrases or clauses.

Below are some examples that illustrate typical adjective phrase patterns (caps designate the HEAD, underlining the complement, and italics the *modifiers*):

FOND

quite FOND

FOND *enough*

FOND of eggs

quite FOND of eggs

The adjective *fond* licenses either no complements or one. If it is clear how someone or something is "fond," as in *a fond farewell* or *a fond memory*, no complement is needed. However, if the noun being modified does not usually have the property of fondness, a complement can provide further information. For instance, the sentence *I am fond* does not make much sense, prompting us to ask, "What are you fond of?" We could add a prepositional phrase for clarification: *I am fond of eggs*. Here, *of eggs* serves as a complement because it provides required information.

We can use the diagnostic test of omission, stacking, and rearrangement to distinguish between complements and modifiers. If we omit *of eggs*, we are left with *I am fond*, which, as we have just seen, does not make sense. We cannot stack similar constituents *(*fond of eggs of coffee)*. Finally, if we cannot stack constituents, there is nothing to rearrange. What if we were to add another prepositional phrase, as in *I am fond of eggs for breakfast*? Here, *for breakfast* would describe the eggs, not someone's fondness. If we posed the question "What are you fond of?", the answer would be "eggs for breakfast." All of this confirms that *of eggs* is a complement licensed by the adjective *fond*.

Adjectives that often take complements include *ready, afraid, proud, sad, reluctant, eager, glad, happy, sorry, liable, likely, certain*, and other words that describe states, emotions, and degrees of modality.

In chapter 4, we learned that adjectives occur in three positions: *attributive* adjectives precede the noun or nominal they modify; *post-positive* adjectives follow the noun or nominal they modify; and *predicate* adjectives follow a verb whose meaning they complete. The same thing holds for adjective phrases. (Again, individual adjectives are really adjective phrases consisting of only a head.) There are attributive, post-positive, and predicate adjective phrases. Generally speaking, attributive adjective phrases tend to be simpler than post-positive and predicate adjective phrases. For example, if we wanted to describe vikings spoiling for battle, we would not call them *eager-to-fight vikings, but *vikings eager to fight*. The presence of the complement *to fight* requires shifting the entire adjective phrase (*eager to fight*) after the noun (*vikings*).

Adverb Phrases

ADVERB PHRASES are headed by adverbs. They rarely take complements, and their complements and modifiers are restricted to a narrower range of structures than other types of phrases. The most common type of adverb phrase complement is the prepositional phrase, as in *The red car crossed the finish line* SIMULTANEOUSLY *with the green one*. Modifiers occurring in adverb phrases will be other adverbs or adverbials. The most common pre-modifiers are intensifying and focusing adverbs, as in *very* QUICKLY or *nearly* NOISELESSLY, while the most common post-modifiers are prepositional phrases.

Whereas the chief function of adjective phrases is to modify noun phrases and nominals, the primary use of adverb phrases is to modify the remaining kinds of phrases – verb phrases, adjective phrases, prepositional phrases, and other adverb phrases – as well as entire clauses. Adverb phrases can also serve as verb phrase complements (*I am here*, *Natalie lives upstairs*). Verb phrase complements will be discussed at greater length in chapter 14 below.

Prepositional Phrases

PREPOSITIONAL PHRASES are headed by a preposition; they always require a complement, the *object of the preposition*. Though they are not usually modified, prepositions that specify relationships or space or time can take adverbial pre-modifiers: *high up the mountain*, *deep below the surface*, *shortly before noon*.

83

Prepositions most often license noun phrases complements; sometimes, adverbs and adverbials (including other prepositional phrases) can serve as complements, as in *until recently*, *like now, until after dinner, out of here*. A few prepositions license adjective complements: *The assassins left them for dead*.

Prepositional phrases most commonly function as adjectivals (when modifying noun phrases or nominals) or adverbials (when modifying any other kind of phrase). In *houses on the mountain, on the mountain* is an adjectival modifying *houses*, but in *I slept on the mountain* it functions as an adverbial of place.

On occasion, a prepositional phrase could belong to either a noun phrase or a verb phrase, requiring some consideration about which structure is being modified or complemented. Usually, context will provide the necessary clue. For instance, in *Bob saw the girl with his bucket*, the prepositional phrase *with his bucket* modifies *the girl*; buckets aren't used for seeing. Likewise, in *Bob saw the moon with his telescope*, the phrase *with his telescope* describes how the moon was seen. Although *Bob saw the girl with his bucket* and *Bob saw the moon with his telescope* contain words of exactly the same class in exactly the same order, the underlying syntax of the sentences differs, as the trees below show. (Both trees employ *triangles* to represent entire phrases, an abbreviation used when it is not important to show the internal structure of a constituent.)

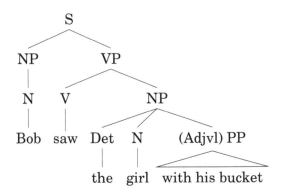

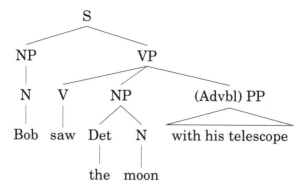

In the first sentence, the adjectival prepositional phrase *with his bucket* occurs under – *is governed by* – the node NP and modifies the noun *girl*. In the second sentence, the adverbial prepositional phrase *with his telescope* is governed by the node VP, indicating that it modifies the verb *saw* (the head of the verb phrase).

More about nested phrases

As noted in chapter 10, phrases can be stacked inside one another. To see how this applies to adjective, adverb, and prepositional phrases, consider the sentence *The book was almost completely free of typos*. Here, *almost completely free of typos* functions as an adjective phrase describing *the book*; we could substitute a single related adjective, such as *error-free*, for the expression: *The book was error-free*. The head of this phrase is the adjective *free*, which licenses the complementary prepositional phrase *of typos*; a "free" book and one "free of typos" are very different things. *Completely* is an adverb phrase consisting of a single adverb modifying *free*, and *almost* in turn qualifies *completely*, so it, too, must be an adverb. Here is a phrase structure tree of the whole sentence:

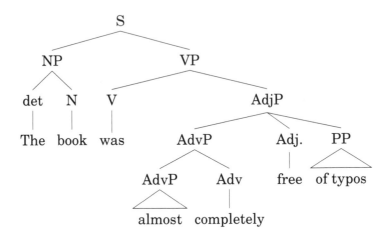

A note on usage

In standard written English, it is best to avoid unnecessary prepositions, as in *where they are at* (compare *where they are*), and *where she is going to* (*where she is going*). In some cases, notably *off of*, you can substitute a single preposition for two: *the design based off of Edison's* can be rewritten *the design based on Edison's*.

Also, a succession of prepositional phrases can bog down your writing. Most sentences can be revised to eliminate at least one of these. *This sentence is a demonstration of the over-use of prepositional phrases in one's writing* can become *This sentence demonstrates the over-use of prepositional phrases; is a demonstration of* can be rephrased as *demonstrates*, and *in one's writing* can simply be eliminated.

Terms, Questions, and Exercises

ADJECTIVE PHRASE, ADVERB PHRASE, PREPOSITIONAL PHRASE.

1. For each underlined group of words in the sentences below, identify the type of phrase, then name the head and any pre-modifiers, post-modifiers, and complements present. If the phrase is an adjective phrase, categorize it as attributive, post-positive, or predicative. Finally, identify the structure the phrase is modifying or completing. (Note that adverb phrases can be embedded within adjective phrases.)

   Example: _Very clever merchants raise their prices slowly_ – _The attributive adjective phrase "very clever" consists of the head "clever" and the pre-modifying adverb "very"; "very clever" modifies "merchants." The adverb phrase "slowly" consists of the head "slowly"; it modifies the verb, "raise."_

   a) The <u>dirty</u> dog barked <u>excitedly</u>.

   b) Lizzy <u>gratefully</u> took the cup of <u>extremely hot</u> cider.

   c) The <u>vividly orange</u> wall attracted attention.

   d) [Challenge.] The general was <u>sure of success</u>.

2. List three prepositional phrases with simple prepositions and two prepositional phrases with complex prepositions. (As we learned in chapter 6, simple prepositions consist of one word, complex prepositions of two or more words.)

3. In the sentences below, identify each prepositional phrase and name the element which it modifies or completes. Also identify each as adjectival or adverbial.

   a) The pile of leaves shifted.

   b) We drove during the downpour.

   c) Someone in the back yelled "fire," causing the crowd to panic.

   d) [Challenge.] In the first half of the second episode of "Dice Tower," the gang discussed _Agricola_.

4. Eliminate any unnecessary prepositions or prepositional phrases in the sentences below:

   a) Where did you park your car at?

   b) She took the whistling kettle off of the burner.

   c) Can you meet with me in the afternoon?

   d) The proposal of the research group met with the approval of the cabinet.

12. Noun Phrases

NOUN PHRASES, which are headed by nouns, show greater structural complexity than adjective, adverb, or prepositional phrases. This is not surprising, given their respective roles. Whereas adjective, adverb, and prepositional phrases serve primarily as *modifiers*, providing optional information about the structures upon which they depend, noun phrases proto-typically fill one of the two required slots within a sentence, that of subject; at the phrase-level, noun phrases often serve as complements, especially in prepositional phrases and verb phrases.

The structure of the noun phrase

The noun phrase's greater complexity expresses itself lies in its structure. In addition to the four familiar components – pre-modifiers, heads, complements, and post-modifiers – noun phrases can also contain two added elements, determiners and pre-determiners. Pre-determiners and determiners always take initial position; the noun phrase's structure can thus be represented as follows:

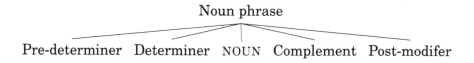

Noun phrase

Pre-determiner Determiner NOUN Complement Post-modifer

In addition to these added elements, noun phrases tend to have more – and a greater variety of – modifiers and complements than adjective, adverb, and prepositional phrases.

As discussed in chapter 4, determiners include articles (*a*, *an*, *the*), possessives (*my*, *her*, *Charlie's*), demonstratives (*this*, *these*, *that*, *those*), indefinites (*some*, *any*, *no*, *every*), and numbers (*one*, *two* ...). Their major function is to signal the noun phrase and to express certain kinds of information, such as definiteness, number, quantity, and proximity. Some determiners can be modified, in which case the modifying word functions as a PRE-DETERMINER. (Because they can be modified, some grammars treat determiners as heads of *determiner phrases*; however, since they are only found in noun phrases, it makes better sense to treat them as noun phrase components.) Some examples of pre-determiners include *all* in *all her friends*, *half* in *half a cup*, and *such* in *such an honor*.

The prototypical noun phrase pre-modifier is the adjective phrase. Because they are modifiers, there is no limit to the number of adjective phrases that can precede the head of a noun phrase. In *beautifully vivid, intensely green malachite*, the noun *malachite* is modified by two adjective phrases:

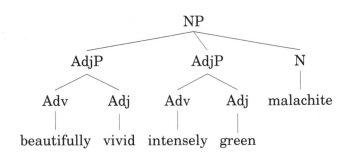

Another common pre-modifier is the embedded noun phrase with adjectival function, as in *garden* PARTY, *police* DOG, or *college* EVENT. Embedded noun phrases, too, can be stacked, as in *dog-sled race*:

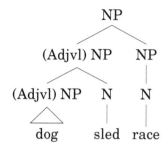

When noun pre-modifiers are nested inside one another, they are usually hyphenated to avoid confusion.

Noun phrases are headed by nouns. Contemporary grammars categorize pronouns as a sub-type of noun, allowing pronouns to head noun phrases. We will follow this convention, while noting that pronouns also differ from nouns in certain ways; for instance, pronouns cannot be pre-modified, and only indefinite pronouns allow post-modification (*anyone present*, but not **she present*).

Some nouns take complements, typically in the form of prepositional phrases or clauses. Words like *fact, claim, belief, completion, failure,* or *possibility* often license complements: *The fact that they juggle katanas amazes me.* The same holds true for nouns describing quantities, such as *abundance, excess, profusion, deficit, scarcity, shortage,* and *want*; some of these nouns, especially in the plural, require complements: *bunches, tons, oodles, wads, reams, scads,* and *gobs.*

Noun phrase post-modifiers include prepositional phrases (*city in the desert*), participial verb phrases (*spectators yelling loudly, boulders hurled by the catapult*), and relative clauses (*plans which we made*).

Nesting in noun phrases

As we saw in the previous chapter, it can be difficult to determine which structure a post-modifier is modifying. This applies not just in cases where a prepositional phrase could be either adverbial or adjectival, but also when it is certainly adjectival. Consider two expressions cited in chapter 10, *books on the third shelf from the top* and *shoes with white laces in her closet*. Superficially, these have an identical structure; in each, a noun (*books* / *shoes*) is followed by two adjectival prepositional phrases (*on the third shelf, from the top* / *with white laces, in her closet*). However, the internal structure of the expressions differs, with the second prepositional phrase of each modifying a different element. In *books on the third shelf from the top, from the top* provides more information about the preceding phrase, *on the third shelf* ("the third shelf as counted from the top down"), whereas in *shoes with white laces in her closet, in her closet* does not modify *with white laces* but *shoes*:

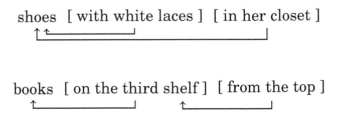

In the first expression, both prepositional phrases modify the head of the noun phrase *shoes*; in the second, the first PP, *on the third shelf*, modifies *books*, whereas the second, *from the top*, modifies *shelf*. This difference is illustrated in the phrase structure trees below:

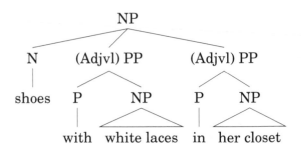

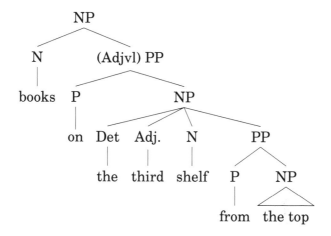

In the first tree, both prepositional phrases directly modify *shoes*. In the second tree, one prepositional phrase (*from the top*) is stacked inside the other (*on the third shelf*).

Identifying noun phrases

Because noun phrases can contain so many different nested elements, it can be difficult to tell where they begin and end. Fortunately, there is an easy way to identify noun phrases. When personal pronouns substitute for a noun phrase, they replace the *entire* phrase, from pre-determiner to post-modifier. To make sure you've correctly identified a sequence of words as noun phrase, try replacing it with a personal pronoun. (Make sure it's a personal pronoun, not an indefinite pronoun or an adverb. Personal pronouns are discussed in chapter 7 above.) For instance, in *The plane taxying down the runway accelerated*, we might suspect that *the plane* is a noun phrase, but **It taxying down the runway accelerated* is an ungrammatical sentence. This is because *taxying down the runway* is a post-modifier describing *the plane*. If we replace the entire phrase, the resulting sentence would be *It accelerated*. Thus, the full noun phrase is *the plane taxying down the runway*. Using the pronoun substitution test, we can also identify another noun phrase (*the runway*) nested inside this one: *The plane taxying down it accelerated.*

A note on usage

The complexity of noun phrases can present problems in SUB-JECT-VERB AGREEMENT. In formal written English, the subject and verb of a clause must agree in number (singular or plural) and person (first, second, or third). When a noun phrase serves as the subject of the clause, it is the head of that phrase – not of a complement or post-modifier – which should determine the number of the verb. Thus, **The use of calculators, cell phones, or other electronic devices are prohibited* should be *The use of calculators, cell phones, or other electronic devices is prohibited*, because the phrase's head (*use*) is singular.

Terms, Questions, and Exercises

NOUN PHRASE, PRE-DETERMINER, SUBJECT-VERB AGREE-MENT.

1. Noun phrases have two unique elements. What are these? In order, what are the six noun phrase elements?

2. What kinds of structures typically function as NP premodifiers? As NP post-modifiers?

3. Use the pronoun substitution test to identify whether the underlined words constitute complete noun phrases.

   a) Five <u>exchange-students from Norway</u> came to <u>our town</u>.

   b) <u>Soundly snoring cats</u> lay <u>upon the sofa</u>.

   c) <u>The book</u> which I read interested <u>Sherry</u>.

4. Use the pronoun substitution test to identify the noun phrases in the following sentences.

   a) The tall trees dropped some of the leaves.

   b) The dog that chased the squirrel barked loudly.

   c) All the top goal-scorers have an instinct for the goal.

5. In the following expressions, identify the *head word* that each underlined prepositional phrase modifies:

   a) cars on the road <u>to town</u>

   b) orcs with swords <u>in the dungeon</u>

   c) friends of my sister <u>from Indianapolis</u>

   d) shoes from a store <u>in Venice</u>

6. In the following sentence, which form of the verb is correct, and why? *A cluster of grapes was / were hanging on the vine.*

13. Verb Phrase Structure

The verb phrase displays even greater complexity than the noun phrase. This complexity manifests itself in both the structure of verbs themselves and also in the number and kinds of complements that they take. Moreover, there are finite and non-finite verb phrases, and these play different roles within a sentence. Because verb phrases are so complex, our discussion of them will be divided into several parts: this chapter gives an overview of the verb phrase and shows how main and helping verbs combine to indicate tense, aspect, and modality; chapter 14 examines verb phrase complements and modifiers; chapter 15 focuses on present participle phrases; chapter 16 discusses infinitive phrases; chapter 17 looks at the passive voice; and chapter 18 treats past participle phrases.

Composition of the verb phrase

The head of the VERB PHRASE is the verb. VERBS are composed of two elements, an *auxiliary* (or *helping*) *verb* and a *main verb*. Even when no helping verb is present, the verb's *tense* is best considered a kind of auxiliary. In addition, the auxiliary (Aux) slot can also contain information about the verb's *modality* (its likelihood or necessity), its duration (the *progressive aspect*), and its relationship in time to another event (the *perfective aspect*). The diagram below illustrates the STRUCTURE OF THE VERB PHRASE:

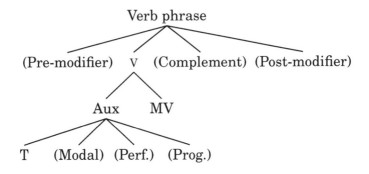

The minimal verb phrase consists of just a verb, that is, *T* (*tense*) and *MV* (the *main verb*): *Bob [snored].*

Tense

In discussing verb tenses, it is important to distinguish between *time* and *tense*. TIME is a natural phenomenon, conventionally divided into *past, present,* and *future,* by which human beings experience reality. TENSE is a grammatical category, expressed through verbs, through which languages make time references. Time and tense are not identical. For example, in *She leaves tomorrow, leaves* shows present tense but future time.

Some languages have elaborate systems of verb inflection that allow nuanced time references, but English inflects main verbs for only two tenses: the *past* and the *present.* As noted in chapter 5, the four verb inflections are third-person singular present, *-s;* the simple past, *-ed;* the past participle, *-n / -ed;* and the present participle, *-ing.* Thus, main verbs on their own can show the present and the simple past; past and present participles are used to make references to time, but only along with helping verbs. Therefore, it is important to distinguish between SIMPLE TENSES, which use only the main verb to make time references, and COMPOUND TENSES, which also use helping verbs to make time references.

In forming compound tenses, English uses the modals *will* or *shall* to reference future time, *be + present participle* (the PROGRESSIVE ASPECT) to indicate *duration*, and *have + past participle* (the PERFECTIVE ASPECT) to show relationships in time to other events or states.

Essentially, English combines tense proper, modals, and the two aspects to provide chronological information about the main verb. We can best think of this information as being part of the auxiliary. Information about tense is not spread evenly across the verb as a whole. For instance, if we wish to locate an action in past time, we can say something like *Daniel smiled*, adding the past-tense morpheme *-ed* to the main verb *smile*. However, we could also say *Daniel could smile*. In the latter sentence, the main verb *smile* is not inflected (**Daniel could smiled*); only the modal verb is inflected for tense. (*Could* is the past form of *can*.) Similarly, *Daniel had been smiling* occurs in past time, but *smiling* is not the past form of *smile*. Again, it is the helping verb – here *has* (past tense *had*) – which bears the inflection for tense.

It turns out that there is a FORMULA FOR PRODUCING VERBS:

$$\text{T} \longrightarrow \text{(M)} \longrightarrow \text{(Perf: } have) \longrightarrow \text{(Prog: } be) \longrightarrow \text{MV}$$

pres. /	∅	+ *-n* / *-ed*	+ *-ing*
past			

Tense (either *present* or *past*) and a main verb are always required; optional elements – modals, the perfective aspect (expressed by a form of *have* and a past participle), and the progressive aspect (expressed by a form of *be* and a present participle) – are indicated by parentheses. The arrows indicate that, moving from left to right, each element influences its direct neighbor. The items with text written below them "pass on" information: *T* passes tense (*present* or *past*), the *Perfective aspect* passes *-n* / *-ed*, and the *Progressive aspect* passes *-ing*. Modals do not influence the next element.

Let us consider a few examples using the main verb *smile*. The simple past tense is formed by "T + MV," with "tense" simply changing the main verb *smile* to *smiled*. Next, we could add the perfective aspect: "T (past) + Perf (*have*) + MV." This gives us the framework *have smile*. Now we apply the information written below, moving left to right: *T (past)* changes *have* to *had* (*had* is the past form of *have*); and the perfective aspect adds *-n / -ed* to the word to the right of *have*, here *smile*, meaning we get *smiled*. Thus, the past perfective form of *smile* is *had smiled*. Finally, let's add the progressive aspect as well: "T (past) + Perf (*have*) + Prog (*be*) + MV." Thus, we begin with the framework *have be smile*. Again, we apply the information written below: *T (past)* changes *have* to *had*; the perfective aspect adds *-n / -ed* to the word to the right of *have*, this time *be*, yielding *been*; and the progressive aspect adds *-ing* to the next word to the right, changing *smile* to *smiling*. Here is a visual representation of the past, past perfective, and past perfective progressive forms of *smile*:

$$T \xrightarrow[past]{} smile = smiled$$

$$T \xrightarrow[past]{} have \xrightarrow[n/ed]{} smile = had\ smiled$$

$$T \xrightarrow[past]{} have \xrightarrow[n/ed]{} be \xrightarrow[ing]{} smile = had\ been\ smiling$$

If we further stipulate that the future tense is indicated by the modal verbs *will* or *shall*, we can generate a table of tenses such as the one shown in 13.1 below.

The different tenses can express a wide range of meanings. Generally speaking, however, the *present tense* is used in situations that obtain around the moment of the utterance; this includes current or recurring events, habits, and universal truths. The present tense can also refer to future situations that are anchored in the present. For instance, in the example cited above, *She leaves tomorrow*, we can infer that though

Tense	Structure	Sample sentence
	Perf. = *have* + *-en* / *-ed*	
	Prog. = *be* + *-ing*	
past	T (past) + MV	I ate
past perf.	T (past) + Perf. + MV	I had eaten
past prog.	T (past) + Prog. + MV	I was eating
past perf. prog.	T (past) + Perf. + Prog. + MV	I had been eating
present	T (pres.) + MV	I eat
present perf.	T (pres.) + Perf. + MV	I have eaten
present prog.	T (pres.) + Prog. + MV	I am eating
present perf. prog.	T (pres.) + Perf. + Prog. + MV	I have been eating
future	T (pres.) + M + MV	I will eat
future perf.	T (pres.) + M + Perf. + MV	I will have eaten
future prog.	T (pres.) + M + Prog. + MV	I will be eating
future perf. prog.	T (pres.) + M + Perf. + Prog. + MV	I will have been eating

Table 13.1.: Verb tenses

"her" departure will take place in the future, it has already been determined now, in the present. The *past tense* is used primarily to describe past events or states, as well as situations contrary to current fact, such as requests (*We hoped you could repeat your story*). The *future tense*, formed with the modals *shall* or *will*, refers to events or states that have not happened but are expected to. The *progressive aspect* describes situations that were, are, or will be ongoing. Finally, the *perfective aspect* applies to states or events seen as completed or to be completed.

A note on usage

Problems with verb tenses occur primarily in the past tenses. When two situations take place in the past and one occurs before the other, informal usage often uses the simple past to describe both: *The bank went up where the old Shell gas station was*. Standard written English uses the *past perfective* to describe the earlier situation: *The bank went up where the old Shell station had been*. This allows the events to be situated in time relative to one another.

Another common problem involves shifting between past and present tense while discussing the same time-frame; the subject happened in the past, but the writer's verbs shift between past and present tenses. This is especially common when the LITERARY PRESENT – writing about the past in present tense – is used: *Shakespeare draws strikingly realistic character portraits. He wrote "Hamlet" between 1599 and 1602. In the character of Hamlet, Shakespeare gives us the best-known portrait of a man plagued by indecision*. Here the first and third sentences use the present tense (*draws, gives*), while the second uses the simple past (*wrote*). To avoid confusing the reader with tense shifts, it is best to stick to one tense. In this case, it would be simplest to use the past throughout: *Shakespeare drew strikingly realistic character portraits. He wrote "Hamlet" between 1599 and 1602. In the character of Hamlet, Shakespeare gave us the best-known portrait of a man plagued by indecision*.

Terms, Questions, and Exercises

VERB PHRASE, STRUCTURE OF VERB PHRASE, TIME, TENSE, SIMPLE TENSES (PRESENT, PAST), COMPOUND TENSES, PERFECTIVE ASPECT, PROGRESSIVE ASPECT, FORMULA FOR PRODUCING VERBS, LITERARY PRESENT.

1. Draw a diagram of the structure of English verb phrases.

2. The verb of a sentence consists of *Aux* and *MV*. What information is always contained in Aux, even when no helping verb is present?

3. Why do some grammarians argue that English has only two tenses? What is the difference between the simple and compound tenses?

4. What is the formula for producing verbs?

5. Write the appropriately tensed version of the following verbs. (*Example: Waves crash, future perfect = will have crashed.*)

   a) *You turn*, past

   b) *You turn*, past perfect

   c) *You turn*, past perfect progressive

6. For each of the following verbs, identify the tense (including aspect). (*Example: Susan had been swimming = past perfect progressive.*)

   a) The lion sleeps tonight.

   b) The lion will sleep tonight.

   c) The lion will have slept tonight.

   d) The lion will have been sleeping tonight.

   e) The lion has been sleeping.

   f) The lion had been sleeping.

   g) The lion slept.

   h) The lion had slept.

7. In the sentences that follow, correct any unnecessary tense shifts: *We drove up to his house. A dog runs out and starts barking. We stayed in the car and waited for him to come out.*

14. Verb Phrase Modifiers and Complements

In this chapter, we will examine the kinds of modifiers and complements found in verb phrases. Before doing so, it will be helpful to take a brief look at the role finite verb phrases play within a sentence.

Sentences, subjects, and predicates

At their most basic level, all ideas have two components, namely a topic and some statement about that topic. In *Bob knows*, *The crowd gave the actors a standing ovation*, and *Flying overseas in July can cost a lot of money*, the topics are *Bob*, *The audience*, and *Flying overseas in July*; the statement made about Bob is that he *knows*, about the audience that they *gave the actors a standing ovation*, and about flying overseas in July that it *can cost a lot of money*.

Just as ideas consist of a topic and a statement, sentences are composed of a *subject* (analogous to the "topic") and a *predicate* (analogous to the "statement about the topic"). We have previously distinguished between grammatical form and function, and this distinction can also help us here. SUBJECT and PREDICATE describe clause-level grammatical functions fulfilled by a particular kind of constituent; the subject function is almost always fulfilled by *noun phrases* or *nominals*, and the predicate function by *verb phrases*. A useful trick for identifying the subject of any sentence is via a TAG QUESTION, a construction added to clauses for confirmation: *Bob knows, doesn't he?* (Who is "he"? *Bob.*) *The crowd gave the actors a standing ovation, didn't it?* (Who is "it"? *The crowd.*) *Flying overseas it July can cost a lot of money, doesn't it?* (What is "it"? *Flying overseas in July.*) Each of these sentences follows the basic *subject + predicate* structure, which, for *Bob knows*, looks like this:

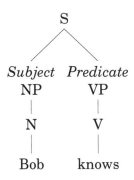

(For simplicity's sake, the internal structure of *V – Aux + MV–* is omitted here.) As this diagram shows, the simplest sentences consist only of a noun, such as *Bob*, and a verb, like *knows*. Of course, sentences can be far more complex than *Bob knows*, and much of this complexity derives from the nature of the English verb phrase – specifically, the various different complements that verbs can take.

Verb phrase modifiers and patterns of complementation

The verb phrase modifiers are adverbs and adverbials. Adverbs occur both as pre-modifiers and post-modifiers; other common post-modifiers include prepositional phrases and dependent clauses.

Verb phrases display five patterns of complementation, each associated with a particular kind of verb. We distinguish between three general categories of main verbs: *linking* verbs, *transitive* verbs, and *intransitive* verbs.

Linking verbs

LINKING (or COPULAR) verbs describe states, processes, or results, and they "link" the subject of the clause and the verb phrase's complement so that the complement restates or describes the subject. A linking verb's complement is therefore called a SUBJECT COMPLEMENT. There are three kinds of subject complements: *adjectives / adjectivals*; *nouns / nominals*; and *adverbs / adverbials*. The prototypical linking verb, *be*, illustrates the different kinds of complementation: *She is tall* (adjective); *Warren Buffett is a famous investor* (noun phrase); and *The ball is in the end-zone* (adverbial). Noun phrase complements of linking verbs are PREDICATE NOMINATIVES, while adjective phrase complements are PREDICATE ADJECTIVES. Common linking verbs include *appear, be, become, get, grow, seem*, and *turn*, as well as verbs pertaining to the senses, such as *feel, look, smell, sound*, and *taste*.

Transitive verbs

The term *transitive verb* derives from Latin *transitivus*, "passing across," whose root also occurs in words like *transit* and *transition*. This is why some grammars state that a transitive verb "passes action" to its complement, or that the complement "receives the action" of the verb. As noted in chapter 5 above, however, verbs do not necessarily convey action, making this a problematic definition; for instance, in *Bob knows Betty* or *Reading requires patience, knows* and *requires* are transitive verbs, but neither describes an action. Therefore, we have to approach the problem differently.

Transitive verbs, like linking verbs, require complements, but the relationship between a transitive verb and its complement (its *direct object*) differs from that of a linking verb and its complement. If we recall that the complement of a linking verb – the subject complement – restates or describes the clause's subject, we can define TRANSITIVE VERBS as taking as complement a direct object which does *not* restate or describe the clause's subject. As will be discussed below, some transitive verbs can also take *indirect objects* and *direct object complements*. An additional difference between linking and transitive verbs is that the linking verbs cannot undergo the passive transformation, whereas all but a very few transitive verbs can (see chapter 17). A DIRECT OBJECT is a noun phrase or nominal that complements a transitive verb. Note that some verbs (e.g., *sneak*, *glance*, and *reside*) require *adverbial* complements; these are not direct objects, which must be noun phrases or nominals.

For now, the easiest way to distinguish between linking and transitive verbs is to apply a simple rule of thumb: if the main verb of a sentence is a form of *to be*, or if *to be* can approximately substitute for the meaning of the main verb, the verb is linking; otherwise, the verb is transitive. For instance, in *The ice cream tasted great*, we can substitute *was* for *tasted* with little change in meaning: *The ice cream was great*. In *The child tasted the ice cream*, however, one cannot substitute *was*: **The child was the ice cream*.

Intransitive verbs

The third kind of verb is the INTRANSITIVE VERB, whose defining characteristic is the lack of a complement. Such verbs "suffice unto themselves" to describe the phenomenon being described. Common intransitive verbs include *appear*, *arrive*, *begin*, *break*, *die*, *go*, *happen*, *start*, *stop*, *swim*, as well as verbs describing common behaviors like *blink*, *cough*, *frown*, *nod*, *laugh*, *smile*, and *smirk*. While intransitive verbs do not have direct object complements, they can take modifying adverbials. **Mike smiled the crowd* is a non-sentence, but we *can* say *Mike smiled at the crowd*; similarly, one does not **arrive the scene*, but one can *arrive on the scene*.

Some verbs are always transitive, others always intransitive. Still others verbs, however, can be either transitive or intransitive: *The movie started* is intransitive (*start* has no complement), but *I started the movie* is transitive (*the movie* is a direct object); *The board broke* is intransitive, but *the Kung Fu master broke the board* is transitive. That is, *start* and *break* can either license no complements, in which case they are intransitive, or a direct object, in which case they are transitive. Linking verbs can also often be used transitively, as illustrated by two sentences cited above, *The ice cream tasted great* (linking) and *The child tasted the ice cream* (transitive). A few verbs, like *smell*, can even manifest all three patterns of complementation: *Mike smells* (intransitive); *Mike smells great* (linking); *Mike smells dinner* (transitive). As these examples show, *smell* can license no complements, a subject complement, or a direct object.

Types of transitive verbs

In addition to the direct object, some transitive verbs can also take other types of complements, a *direct object complement* or an *indirect object*. As its name implies, a DIRECT OBJECT COMPLEMENT completes the meaning of the verb's direct object. Direct object complements can be nominal (*The panel declared him the winner*), adjectival (*Star Wars made George Lucas famous*), or adverbial (*She put the pizza in the oven*). In each case, the object complement cannot be omitted: **The panel declared him*; **Star Wars made George Lucas* (to "make" someone is not the same as making someone famous); and **She put the pizza*. To-infinitives and participial phrases often serve as object complements, as illustrated by sentences like *I want you to memorize this* (*you* is the direct object, *to memorize this* the object complement) and *He saw the train coming* (*train* is the direct object, *coming* the object complement).

The second type of complement is the INDIRECT OBJECT, a nominal that occurs either without preposition after the verb and before the direct object, or with preposition and after both the verb and the direct object; the indirect object usually represents the recipient or goal of an action or event. For instance, the underlined words in the following sentences are indirect objects: *I threw him the ball*; *I baked her a cake*; *He reserved me a seat*; *She showed her the turtle*; and *I saved him some ice cream*. Indirect objects can be moved before or after the direct object. Thus, the preceding sentences can also be written *I threw the ball to him*; *I baked a cake for her*; *He reserved a seat for me*; *She showed the turtle to her*; and *I saved some ice cream for him*. This does not work with object complements (**The panel declared the winner for him*, **Star Wars made famous to George Lucas*) or prepositional phrases serving as modifiers (*I took him to the farm* cannot turn into **I took the farm him* or **I took him farm*). Verbs that take only a direct object are MONOTRANSITIVE; ones with a direct object and an indirect object are DITRANSITIVE; and ones with a direct object and object complement are COMPLEX TRANSITIVE.

Table 14.1 lists the five types of verb phrase complementation patterns, with the most important sub-types indicated and a sample sentence illustrating each. (Patterns 3, 4, and 5 are all transitive patterns.)

You should familiarize yourself with the five different patterns. They also occur in non-finite verb phrases, so we will encounter them again in the coming chapters.

A note on usage

You may have been given the advice to use "strong" verbs in your writing. Why do verbs matter so much, and what exactly makes a verb "strong"?

As we've seen, the verb phrase manifests the greatest complexity of all phrase types. The verb largely determines a sentence's shape. "Strong" verbs engage the reader's attention through specificity and variation (a principle we will discuss in chapter 29). To make your verbs stronger, start by identifying

Verb type	Sample sentence
1. Intransitive no complement	She SLEPT.

2. Linking
  a. nominal complement
  b. adjectival complement
  c. adverbial complement
	I BECAME a student.
	I SEEM silly.
	I AM inside.

3. Monotransitive direct object only	He SEES William.
4. Ditransitive indirect + direct object	He BROUGHT me the check.

5. Complex transitive
  a. direct object + nominal comp.
  b. direct object + adjectival comp.
  c. direct object + adverbial comp.
	They CALLED him captain.
	They DEEMED her worthy.
	They TOOK me upstairs.

Table 14.1.: Verb complementation patterns

riffs of *be* used as linking verb and rewrite the sentences that contain them. You can often substitute a closely related verb for *be* + complement. For example, the sentence *This is a circumstance which is not tolerable for us* contains two instances of *be* as linking verb; it can be rephrased so as to eliminate both: *We cannot tolerate this circumstance.* (*This circumstance* takes the place of *This is a circumstance which* and *tolerate* replaces *is tolerable*).

Terms, Questions, and Exercises

SUBJECT, PREDICATE, TAG QUESTION, LINKING (COPULAR) VERB, SUBJECT COMPLEMENT, PREDICATE NOMINATIVE, PREDICATE ADJECTIVE, TRANSITIVE VERB, DIRECT OBJECT, INTRANSITIVE VERB, DIRECT OBJECT COMPLEMENT, INDIRECT OBJECT, MONOTRANSITIVE VERB, DITRANSITIVE VERB, COMPLEX TRANSITIVE VERB.

1. What two elements are obligatory in all clauses?

2. Use tag questions to identify the subjects of the following sentences:

    a) Appearances can be deceiving.

    b) My orange cat ate the kibble.

    c) Driving on a gravel road at 60 miles per hour is dangerous.

3. Identify the underlined phrases below as subject complements, direct objects, or modifiers. Then, identify each verb (in small caps) as linking, transitive, or intransitive.

    a) Pet iguanas MAKE interesting pets.

    b) Squirrels MAKE nests in trees.

    c) I LOOKED at the hill.

    d) I LOOKED him in the eyes.

    e) I LOOKED angry.

    f) You WINKED at me.

4. In the sentences below, identify the underlined element as an indirect object, an object complement, or an adverbial modifier.

    a) Mike sings songs in the shower.

    b) Ellie sent a card to him.

    c) We declared them the winners.

    d) She taught me those moves.

5. For the sentences below, identify 1. the main verb that heads the verb phrase, 2. Aux (including *tense*), 3. any verb phrase complements, including their types (*predicate nominative, predicate adjective, adverbial complement of linking verb, direct object, indirect object,* and *direct object*

complement), and 4. any verb phrase modifiers (adverbs and adverbials).

   a) She rode her red bicycle to the school.

   b) We will have declared them the winners.

   c) Pet iguanas can make interesting pets.

6. In the sentences below, identify *be* used as linking verb and rewrite the sentences that contain them to eliminate at least half. (If you can substitute a closely related verb for *be* + complement, do so.)

   There is a debate among educators whether standardized tests are good for helping students to learn. Some teachers are inclined to see them as necessary, while others are of the opinion that they are harmful to students' motivation to learn.

15. Present Participle Phrases

NON-FINITE VERB PHRASES are among the most common structures in English; they convey the same kind of information communicated by verbs, but they lack AUX and typically function as nominals, adjectivals, or adverbials. The ability of verb phrases to act like other kinds of phrases adds versatility to language, allowing us to say things like *Driving at night is challenging*. Using pronoun substitution, we could rewrite this sentence *It is challenging*, showing that the verb phrase *driving at night* functions as a nominal; *challenging* is an adjectival that derives from the verb *challenge*. There are two major kinds of non-finite verb phrases, *participial phrases* and *infinitive phrases*. Participial phrases can be divided into *present participle* (*-ing*) phrases and *past participle* (*-n / -ed*) phrases, while infinitive phrases can be categorized as *to-infinitive* and *bare-infinitive phrases*. This chapter examines present participle phrases, chapter 16 discusses infinitive phrases, and chapter 18 covers past participle phrases.

The structure of present participle phrases

PRESENT PARTICIPLE PHRASES are verb phrases headed by a present participle and lacking AUX. Since they do not have AUX, present participle phrases cannot be preceded by modals (**Could driving at night is challenging*) and they lack tense

(T). To clarify the latter point, although participial phrases are headed by a "present" or a "past" participle, these communicate aspect only. In the sentence *I finished raking the leaves*, "raking" does not take place in the present; the activity was ongoing (the progressive aspect, *raking*) in the past (*finished*). Likewise, in *Kegan will realize that peeling 10,000 potatoes is not much fun*, Kegan's realization takes place in the future, though *peeling 10,000 potatoes* is a "present" participle phrase.

As verb phrases, present participle phrases can employ the full array of modifiers and complements associated with verb phrases. As discussed in the previous chapter, there are five patterns of verb complementation: 1. intransitive verb without complement; 2. linking verb + subject complement; 3. transitive verb + direct object; 4. transitive verb + indirect direct object + direct object; and 5. transitive verb + direct object + object complement. These same patterns also pertain to non-finite verb phrases. Table 15.1 below reproduces the one from chapter 14, but adds present participle phrases in the sample sentences, with the phrase itself marked off by square brackets.

The simplest present participle phrases are those based on pattern 1, because they have no complements. One-word *-ing* phrases like *sleeping, smiling, snoring, skiing*, and so on, are verb phrases consisting only of a head.

The function of present participial phrases

Present participle phrases often act as adjectivals. One-word present participle phrases most often function as noun-phrase pre-modifiers (*the blinking light*), more complex ones as post-modifiers (*the light blinking at regular intervals*). Present participle phrases can also precede the entire noun phrase they modify (including determiners): *Blinking at regular intervals,*

Verb type	Sample sentence
1. Intransitive no complement	*She enjoyed* [SLEEPING].

2. Linking
   a. nominal complement
   b. adjectival complement
   c. adverbial complement
	Upon [BECOMING *a student*], *I rejoiced.*
	I like [SEEMING *silly*].
	[BEING *inside*], *I heard the noise.*

3. Monotransitive direct object only	[SEEING *William*] *made him smile.*
4. Ditransitive indirect + direct object	*He delayed* [BRINGING *me the check*].

5. Complex transitive
   a. direct object + nom. comp.
   b. direct object + adj. comp.
   c. direct object + adv. comp.
	[CALLING *him captain*] *was premature.*
	[DEEMING *her worthy*], *they agreed.*
	After [TAKING *me upstairs*], *they waited.*

Table 15.1.: Present participle verb phrase complementation

the light warned of danger. Present participle phrases with adverbial function are comparatively rare. In *I completed the test racing through the questions*, the *-ing* phrase *racing through the questions* acts as an adverb of manner, describing how the test was completed. Its adverbial nature can be confirmed by the following tests: it answers the question "How?"; one can substitute a single related adverb, such as *quickly* (*I completed the test quickly*); and the phrase can be moved to the beginning of the sentence (*Racing through the questions, I completed the test*). Again, adverbial present participle phrase are comparatively rare; when they are used to express adverbial meaning, present participle phrases are more often nominal objects of a prepositional phrase (for instance, *by racing through the questions*).

Most commonly, present participle phrases act as nominals, in which case they are called GERUNDS. Gerunds can fulfill any role typically played by noun phrases, including *subject, direct object, indirect object, subject complement*, and *object of a preposition*.

Distinguishing present participle phrases from finite verb phrases

Non-finite verb phrases can be nested inside finite verb phrases. For instance, *I like being alone* consists of a subject (NP, *I*) and a predicate (VP, *like being alone*). The verb phrase is type 3: trans. verb (*like*) + direct object (*being alone*). The direct object is a non-finite verb phrase of type 2: linking verb (*being*) + subj. complement (*alone*). The phrase structure tree for this sentence is:

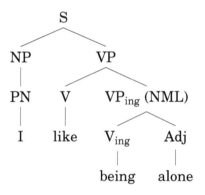

Although such sentences appear complicated, it is not difficult to discern their underlying structure. Since a finite verb phrase is headed by a verb consisting of AUX + *main verb*, we can simply check whether the structure in question answers to this description: *like* can be analyzed as *T (present)* + *like*, meeting the requirements of a finite verb; *being*, however, lacks *aux* (there is no tense marker), and therefore cannot be a finite verb.

In analyzing the structure of sentences that contain non-finite verb phrases, it helps to break down each clause into subject and predicate. In chapter 14, we learned to use the tag-question test to identify the subject of a clause; once we have done so, we can isolate its predicate as well. The left-most main verb will head the verb phrase acting as predicate. Let us try this with two sample sentences to see the process in action:

Melanie enjoys exercising. Tag question: *She enjoys exercising, doesn't she?* Who is "she" (the subject of the clause)? Melanie. In answer to the question *Melanie what?*, we would reply *enjoys exercising.* This verb phrase is the sentence's predicate, and it is headed by *enjoys*, its left-most main verb. *Exercising* is a present participle phrase acting as nominal (direct object) complement.

Alexandre Dumas, author of "The Count of Monte Christo," began writing fiction in the 1820s. Tag question: *Alexandre Dumas, author of "The Count of Monte Christo," began writing fiction in the 1820s, didn't he?* Who is "he" (and therefore the subject of the clause)? *Alexandre Dumas, author of the "The Count of Monte Christo."* To identify the predicate, we ask *He what?*, to which the answer is *Began writing fiction in the 1820s.* This verb phrase is headed by *began*, its left-most main verb. This is a type 3 verb whose direct object is the present participle phrase *writing fiction in the 1820s.* The present participle phrase is also type 3, trans. verb (*writing*) + direct object (*fiction*), with an adverbial prepositional phrase (*in the 1820s*).

A note on usage

When they act as nominals, present participle phrases are sometimes preceded by determiners, as in *the sinking of the Titanic.* Such constructions have the underlying form *determiner + present participle phrase*, the whole functioning as a nominal. Possessive determiners can occur as well, like in the sentences *Michael's passing the bar exam was cause for celebration* or *Mary's arriving late nearly spoiled the surprise.* The non-possessive variants *Michael passing the bar exam was cause for celebration* and *Mary arriving late nearly spoiled the surprise* are common in informal usage.

Formal written English prefers the possessive form, which often clarifies an expression's intended meaning. *Adam did not* *like the <u>woman</u> sitting in front of him* is ambiguous; he either dislikes *the woman* or the fact that she was *sitting in front of him* (perhaps because he was in a movie theater and she was wearing a hat). If the latter is intended, it would be preferable to write *Adam did not like the <u>woman's</u> sitting in front of him*.

Terms, Questions, and Exercises

NON-FINITE VERB PHRASE, PRESENT PARTICIPLE PHRASE, GERUND.

1. What is the defining characteristic of non-finite verb phrases? What three syntactic roles can non-finite verb phrases play?

2. In the following sentences, first identify the present participle phrases, then describe how they function (as nominal, adjectival, or adverbial):

    a) Eating ice cream before dinner will ruin your appetite.

    b) Planes departing Boston's Logan airport encountered heavy turbulence.

    c) I enjoy taking long walks in the morning.

    d) Credited with shooting down 352 enemy aircraft, Erich Hartmann is the most successful flying "ace" of all time.

    e) We crossed the river riding on horseback.

3. What are the five common patterns of verb complementation? Form one present participle phrase using each of the patterns, labeling the different complements.

4. In formal written English, would it preferable to write *I appreciate your loaning your notes to me* or *I appreciate you loaning your notes to me*? Why?

16. Infinitive Phrases

Infinitives come in two varieties, the bare infinitive and the to-infinitive. The BARE INFINITIVE, the unmarked form of a verb, is sometimes also known as the "dictionary form" of the verb (the headword by which it is listed); the bare infinitive form occurs after modal verbs (e.g., *He might disappear*) and in imperative and interrogative clauses (*Will she be there? Be silent!*). *Bare infinitive phrases* are found in a few contexts, including as object complements licensed by certain verbs: *feel, have, hear, help, let, make, notice, observe, see,* and *watch* (for instance, *I had him drive home, She watched me make the shot*).

To-infinitive phrases

TO-INFINITIVE PHRASES – phrases headed by *to* + bare infinitive – occur in a wider variety of contexts than bare infinitive phrases. Like present participle phrases, they can function as any of the three other major classes, that is, as nominals (*I want to win*), adjectivals (*two ways to win*), or adverbials (*To win, one must have a plan*). As nominals, to-infinitive phrases can perform the typical NP roles of subject (*To learn requires concentration*), subject complement (*My goal is to learn*), direct object (*I want to learn*), and direct object complement (*He wants her to learn*). To-infinitive phrases can also complement other constituents, such as adjectives (*eager to learn, ready to go*) and pronouns (*someone to love, everyone to leave*). To distinguish to-infinitive phrases from prepositional phrases, remember that, when acting as a preposition, *to* will be followed by the object of the preposition – typically a noun phrase – not an infinitive.

Present participle and to-infinitive phrases serve similar functions, but it is possible to draw some general distinctions between them. These are tendencies rather than iron-clad rules, but they are still helpful. In particular, three differences emerge: first, present participle phrases more often function as *adjectivals* than as *adverbials*, whereas the reverse holds true for infinitive phrases; second, when functioning as nominals, present participles are more likely to describe an *actual situation* while infinitives more often refer to *conditionals, hypotheticals*, and *goals*; and finally, again with respect to nominals, present participle phrases more often function as *subjects* and infinitives more frequently as *objects*. These points help us to understand how, despite some overlap in the roles they play, the two major types of non-finite verb phrases complement one another as well.

The structure of infinitive phrases

Because they are verb phrases, infinitive phrases make use of the five common patterns of verb-phrase complementation, as illustrated in table 16.1 below. (Like table 15.1, it is based on the patterns of verb phrase complementation exemplified in table 14.1.)

As verbs, infinitives are modified by adverbs or adverbials, as in *I hesitate* TO LEAVE *now* or *He wanted* TO STUDY *in the evening*. If it is not clear which element the adverb(ial) is modifying – here, *hesitate* or *to leave* and *wanted* or *to study* – we must determine which head word governs it. In the first sentence, *now* describes *leaving*, not *hesitating*; therefore, it modifies *to leave*. (If *now* were to modify *hesitate*, the sentence would read *I now hesitate to leave*.) Similarly, in the second sentence, *in the evening* describes *studying* rather than *wanting*. (The prepositional phrase would modify *wanted* in a sentence

Verb type	Sample sentence
1. Intransitive no complement	*She likes* [TO SLEEP].

2. Linking
    a. nominal complement
    b. adjectival complement
    c. adverbial complement
	I want [TO BECOME <u>*a student*</u>].
	I hate [TO SEEM <u>*silly*</u>].
	I love [TO BE <u>*inside*</u>].

3. Monotransitive direct object only	[TO SEE <u>*William*</u>] *made him smile.*
4. Ditransitive indirect + direct object	*I would like him* [TO BRING <u>*me*</u> <u>*the check*</u>].

5. Complex transitive
    a. direct object + nom. comp.
    b. direct object + adj. comp.
    c. direct object + adv. comp.
	They hesitated [TO CALL <u>*him*</u> <u>*captain*</u>].
	They pretended [TO DEEM <u>*her*</u> <u>*worthy*</u>].
	They wanted [TO TAKE <u>*me*</u> <u>*upstairs*</u>].

Table 16.1.: Infinitive phrase complementation

like *In the evening, he wanted to study.*)

One special use of the infinitive phrase occurs in expressions that pair an interrogative with a following to-infinitive: *what to do*, *whom to call*, *where to park*, *when to leave*, and so on. In these *interrogative infinitive phrases*, the interrogative word replaces an equivalent structure and is then moved to the beginning of the phrase. For instance, *what to do* has the underlying pattern *to do something*; *whom to call* comes from *to call someone*, and *where to park* derives from *to park somewhere*. Interrogative infinitive phrases are nominals.

To-infinitive clauses

As we have seen, to-infinitive phrases are non-finite verb phrases that act as nominals, adjectivals, or adverbials. In one case, however, they can also function as predicates, namely in TO-INFINITIVE CLAUSES; these follow the pattern *for* + subject + to-infinitive phrase. To-infinitive clauses are dependent clauses, with *for* acting as a subordinator. For example, in *For the economy to improve, the unemployment rate must drop*, the clause *for the economy to improve* is a dependent to-infinitive clause; *for* is the subordinator, *the economy* the clause's subject, and *to improve* its predicate (note, however, that *to improve* still lacks AUX). The clause has adverbial function, describing the condition necessary for the economy to improve. We will study subordinate clauses in the next unit. For now, the important point to remember is that to-infinitive phrases can act as predicates in the construction *for* + subject + to-infinitive phrase, the whole constituting a *to-infinitive clause*.

A note on usage

Few points of English usage have caused more controversy than the SPLIT INFINITIVE, which occurs when an adverb or adverbial is inserted between *to* and its infinitive, as in Star Trek's *to boldly go where no man has gone before*. In the nineteenth century, prescriptive grammarians coined a rule forbidding split infinitives because Latin infinitives are formed by inflections (*amas* "you love," *amare* "to love"); in other words, Latin infinitives are always single words. Though by no means all authorities agreed that this rule made sense, teachers nevertheless attempted to enforce it.

Writers, however, have always ignored the rule. Among nineteenth-century infinitive-splitters are many of the celebrated novelists and poets of the age, including Samuel Taylor Coleridge, Sir Walter Scott, John Keats, Herbert Spencer, Anthony Trollope, George Eliot, Arthur Conan Doyle, and Mark Twain.

With the growing recognition that the rules of Latin should not be indiscriminately applied to English, injunctions against the split infinitive have become rare. Today most usage guides permit placing an adverb between the *to* and its infinitive, provided that the resulting construction is clear.

Terms, Questions, and Exercises

BARE INFINITIVE, TO-INFINITIVE PHRASE, TO-INFINITIVE
CLAUSE, SPLIT INFINITIVE.

1. What is the difference between a bare infinitive and a to-infinitive? In what context do bare infinitives commonly occur? Name three verbs that often take bare infinitive phrases as complements.

2. What different syntactic roles do to-infinitive verb phrases typically play?

3. In the following sentences, first identify the infinitive phrases, then identify which of the five verb phrase patterns each infinitive phrase employs:

   a) To delay is to fail.

   b) Anthony wanted to buy his friend a present.

   c) Mariah made her stop the car.

   d) They will need to name someone chancellor.

   e) The colonists desired to be free of British rule.

4. What is a to-infinitive clause? Give an example. What is unusual about the role that the infinitive phrase plays within a to-infinitive clause?

5. In the sentences below, identify the to-infinitive phrase and state whether or not it is split. For split infinitives, rewrite the sentence so that the infinitive is no longer split (where possible).

   a) She wanted to quickly finish her chores.

   b) Eventually, I'd like to replace those windows.

   c) Our next quarter earnings are projected to more than double.

17. Passive Verbs

Consider the following sentence pairs: a. *She is throwing the ball* and b. *The ball is being thrown by her*; a. *I had written a book* and b. *A book had been written by me*; and a. *He will dismiss the case* and b. *The case will be dismissed by him*. All of the b. sentences employ the PASSIVE VOICE, containing a passive verb. The a. sentences, on the other hand, use the ACTIVE VOICE, meaning that they do not contain a passive verb. This chapter will examine how the b. sentences are formed through the *passive transformation*.

The passive transformation

Let's look at the relationship between the sentence pairs above. In each pairing, both sentences contain two noun phrases and a verb (which is active in the first sentence and passive in the second). Placing the sentences side by side will allow us to see what is happening:

NP_1 + (Active) <u>Verb</u> + NP_2	NP_2 + (Passive) <u>Verb</u> + (*by* NP_1)
She <u>is throwing</u> the ball	*The ball <u>is being thrown</u> (by her)*
I <u>had written</u> a book	*The book <u>had been written</u> (by me)*
He <u>will dismiss</u> the case	*The case <u>will be dismissed</u> (by him)*

Focusing first on the noun phrases, we can see that the direct objects in the active sentences (NP_2) become the subjects of the passive sentences; conversely, the active sentences' subjects (NP_1) are moved after the passive verb and embedded in a *by* prepositional phrase. In the active sentences, both NPs are required (*Is throwing the ball, *She is throwing), but this is not the case in the passive ones (The ball is being thrown). Thus, the passive sentence's post-verbal prepositional phrase – containing the active sentence's subject – is optional.

The a. and b. sentences also show a systematic difference in verb forms. Here is a side-by-side comparison, with the active verbs on the left and the passive verbs on the right:

is throwing / is being thrown
had written / had been written
will dismiss / will be dismissed

Two points emerge. First, while the active main verbs appear in a variety of forms – throwing is the present participle, written the past participle, and dismiss the infinitive form – the passive main verbs are all past participles (thrown, written, and dismissed). Second, in the active verb phrases the main verb is preceded by different auxiliaries (is, had, and will), but the words immediately preceding the main verb in the passive verb phrases are all forms of be (being, been, and be). We can conclude from this that the passive transformation adds be + -n / -ed to the verb. As we recall from chapter 13, the formula for producing (active) verbs is:

$$T \longrightarrow (M) \longrightarrow (\text{Perf: } have) \longrightarrow (\text{Prog: } be) \longrightarrow MV$$

pres. / ∅   + -n / -ed   + -ing
past

To also take into account the passive voice, we will now add the PASSIVE VERB MARKER, be + -n / -ed, before MV (highlighted in the rectangle):

$$T \longrightarrow (M) \longrightarrow (\text{Perf: } have) \longrightarrow (\text{Prog: } be) \longrightarrow \boxed{(\text{Pass: } be)} \longrightarrow MV$$

pres. / ∅   + -n / -ed   + -ing   + -n / -ed
past

To see this in action, we can revisit the table of verb tenses from chapter 13; to avoid duplicating the whole table, a look at the past tense should suffice. The result is displayed in table

	Active	Passive
past	T (past) + MV *threw*	T (past) + Pass + MV *was thrown*
past perf	T (past) + Perf + MV *had thrown*	T (past) + Perf + Pass + MV *had been thrown*
past prog	T (past) + Prog + MV *was throwing*	T (past) + Prog + Pass + MV *was being thrown*
past perf prog	T (past) + Perf + Prog + MV *had been throwing*	T (past) + Perf + Prog + Pass + MV *had been being thrown*

Table 17.1.: Structure of active and passive verbs

17.1, which confirms that, to change a verb's voice from active to passive, we simply insert *be* + *-n / -ed* prior to the main verb.

One further point about the nature of passive verbs remains to be discussed. It turns out that almost all transitive verbs verbs can be made passive, while linking and intransitive verbs generally cannot. *He snores* cannot become **Snored is by him*, nor can *She is tall* turn into **Tall is being by her*. Only a very few transitive verbs cannot become passive; these include *cost, have, lack, like, resemble, suit,* and *want*. (One can say *It costs five dollars, She has a nice laptop,* and *I like strawberries,* but not **Five dollars is costed by it, *A nice laptop is had by her,* or **Strawberries are liked by me*.) The non-transitive verbs that can be made passive will be discussed below in the section on prepositional passives.

Putting together all of the above, we can now define the PASSIVE TRANSFORMATION: a sentence with a transitive main verb can be made passive by 1. Turning the direct object into the subject of the transformed sentence; 2. either eliminating the subject of the active sentence or prefacing it with *by* and moving it after the verb; and 3. inserting *be* + *-n / -ed* before the main verb.

Identifying passive verbs

A passive sentence can be reverted to its active form by reversing the steps of the passive transformation: 1. cut *be* + *-n* / *-ed* (while retaining tense); 2a. if the sentence identifies an agent in a phrase that begins with *by*, cut *by* and move the remaining phrase to the subject position; 2b. if the sentence does *not* identify an agent in a phrase that begins with *by*, insert a place-holder pronoun like *someone* or *something*; and 3. turn the old subject into a direct object by moving it after the verb. Any sentence which cannot undergo the reversal of the passive transformation cannot be passive. This procedure can be used to identify passive verbs.

Let's see this in action. Which of the following sentences are passive? 1. *They were walking along the beach*; 2. *Simon received his diploma in the mail*; 3. *This procedure can be used to identify passive verbs*; 4. *They had left the rest for him*; 5. *Annabelle was bored*; 6. *We will be annoyed by the delay*.

The main verb of sentence 1, *walking*, does not have the *-n* / *-ed* form, so the sentence *cannot* be passive.

In sentence 2, the main verb does look like it could be a past participle (though it is actually the simple past), but the preceding form of *be* is missing, so we cannot cut *be* + *-n* / *-ed*; sentence 2 also cannot be passive.

The verb of sentence 3, *can be used*, has both a past participle (*used*) and a preceding form of be (*be*); cutting *be* + *-n* / *-ed* leaves *can use*. There is no agent identified in a *by* phrase, so we insert a placeholder (*someone* / *something*) as subject of the new sentence. Finally, we take the current subject, *this procedure*, and make it the direct object of the new sentence. Thus, the active version of sentence 3 is *Someone can use this procedure to identify passive verbs*. All three steps of the reverse passive transformation work; therefore, the original sentence 3 *is* passive.

Sentence 4 has the verb *had left*, which cannot be passive; like sentence 2, it has no form of *be*.

Sentences 5 (*Annabelle was bored*) and 6 (*We will be annoyed by the delay*) are trickier. Both have *be* + *-n* / *-ed* in the verb: *was bored* and *(will) be annoyed*; removing this leaves *bore(s)* and *will annoy*, respectively. Sentence 5 does not state an agent in a *by* phrase, so we insert the placeholder *someone* / *something* as subject of the new sentence; sentence 6 does have a *by* phrase (*by the delay*), so we strike *by* and move *the delay* to the subject position in the new sentence. The current subjects, *Annabelle* in 5 and *we* in 6, become direct objects. After the three steps, sentence 5 becomes *Someone* / *something bored Annabelle* and sentence 6 *The delay will annoy us*. Both original sentences are passive.

Stative passives

Verb phrases such as the one in sentence 5, *was bored*, which combine *be* and a past participle with an adjectival meaning, are STATIVE PASSIVES, passive constructions that describe states of being. Some grammars regard these as "false passives," construing *was bored* not as the passivized version of *bore* but as *be* + *predicate adjective*, similar to *Annabelle was intelligent* or *Annabelle was tall*. However, the distinction between *be* + *participial adjective* and *passive be* + *past participle* does not withstand scrutiny. If we were to add an agent *by* phrase to the original sentence, yielding something like *Annabelle was bored by the movie*, the same grammars that would categorize *Annabelle was bored* as a "false" passive would classify *Annabelle was bored by the movie* as a "true" passive expression. But we have already seen that many unequivocally passive expressions omit the *by* phrase; if these are genuine passives, it makes no sense to regard a sentence like *Annabelle is bored* a false one.

Any sentence that can undergo a reversal of the passive transformation is passive. This does include expressions like *Annabelle was bored*, as well as many others: *The exhibit is closed*; *The runners were tired*; *A window has been broken*; and so on. All of these have active equivalents: *Someone / something closed the exhibit* (e.g., the museum staff); *Someone / something tired the runners* (such as running up the hill); *Someone / something has broken a window* (perhaps a rock). Although these sentences express states of being (being *stative passives*), they are still passive.

Passive *get*

PASSIVE GET constructions feature *get* + -*n* / -*ed* rather than *be* + -*n* / -*ed*. They generally occurs in informal expressions such as *The home team got hammered by the visitors* or *The flight will get delayed*. (Compare *The home team was hammered by the visitors* and *The flight will be delayed*.) Both sentences have active equivalents: *The visitors hammered the home team* and *[Someone / something] will delay the flight*). Passive *get* also occurs in certain idiomatic expressions like *get caught*, *get married*, and *get paid*.

Prepositional passives

As mentioned above, it is usually the case that only transitive verbs can be made passive. The exception to this rule are PREPOSITIONAL PASSIVES, wherein the object of a prepositional phrase takes the place of NP$_2$. This results in structures such as *They were laughed at* (from active *Someone laughed at them*), *The bed was slept in* (from active *Someone slept in the bed*), and *The museum was broken into* (from active *Someone broke into the museum*). Note that this does not work in all cases. For instance, *She frowned in confusion* cannot be made passive (**Confusion was frowned in*), nor can *His mood improved after dinner* (**Dinner was improved after*).

A note on usage

Most style guides counsel writers to avoid using the passive voice whenever possible. However, passive verbs do have their uses.

As we have seen, passive constructions shift the object of a transitive verb to subject position, while the former subject is either moved after the verb or even omitted. *I took three measurements* becomes *Three measurements were taken (by me)*. There are three related reasons why an author might want to do this: to emphasize a sentence's most important idea; to project objectivity; or to engage in *hedging*.

Normally a sentence has two rhetorical peaks: its opening and its ending. Of these, the more important – the *primary focus* – is the opening. In an active sentence, the opening typically identifies the agent – in the sentence above, *I*. The passive version, on the other hand, opens with *three measurements*.

Extending this point a bit further, we can see that the active sentences tend to be more "subjective," the passive ones more "objective." The agent of an active sentence is relegated to a secondary position, or even entirely eliminated, in a passive one.

Finally, eliminating a sentence's agent allows writers to engage in HEDGING, that is, qualifying the force of an assertion. If we believe that a statement is probably true, but lack absolute proof, we can use passive expressions like *it is believed* or *it is assumed* to hedge our bets: *It is believed that Shakespeare acted in his own plays*.

Use of the passive voice entails certain risks. Depersonalized and hedged expressions can sound dry and lacking in conviction. Because they often omit the agent, passive sentences can also be hard to read; even a short passage abounding in passive verbs becomes difficult to navigate. Writers must weigh the potential gains of using the passive voice – projecting a careful and objective persona – against the drawbacks of potentially boring or confusing the reader.

Terms, Questions, and Exercises

PASSIVE VOICE, ACTIVE VOICE, PASSIVE VERB MARKER, PAS-
SIVE TRANSFORMATION, STATIVE PASSIVE, PASSIVE "GET,"
HEDGING.

1. What is the passive verb marker?

2. State the three steps of the passive transformation.

3. Write the complete version of the verb formula (which includes the passive marker).

4. For each of the sentences below, write the passive version if possible, placing the *by* + agent phrase in parentheses. If the sentence cannot be made passive, write "no passive" and identify the kind of verb (that is, *intransitive* or *linking*). Some examples: *I made a mistake – A mistake was made (by me); Larry snores loudly – no passive; "snores" is intransitive.*

   a) "Teddy" Roosevelt was the 26th president of the United States.

   b) He led the Republican party from 1901 to 1909.

   c) Roosevelt went on Safari in Africa in 1909.

   d) He founded the Progressive "Bull Moose" party in 1912.

5. Identify each sentence below as passive or active. If it is passive, write the active equivalent, supplying [*Someone / something*] as subject if no agent is identified in a *by* phrase.

   a) Harrison is cycling along the canal.

   b) The proposal was carefully considered.

   c) The students progressed rapidly.

d) Some space exploration is being conducted by private companies.

18. Past Participle Phrases

PAST PARTICIPLE PHRASES are non-finite verb phrases headed by a past participle. They resemble present participle phrases in all points except three.

To illustrate the first of these differences, compare the expressions *the man eating a dinner*, which contains an *-ing* phrase (*eating a dinner*), and *the man eaten at dinner*, which incorporates an *-n/-ed* phrase (*eaten at dinner*). Despite their similar appearance, these phrases have one important difference, namely whether the man is consuming or being consumed. After learning about passive verbs, we can identify this difference as involving the verb's voice: *eating* is active and *eaten* is passive. Thus, non-finite verb phrases headed by present participles are active, whereas those headed by past participles are predominantly passive. (Those whose meaning is not obviously passive, like *the man tired of take-out dinners* or *the museum wing closed for renovation*, contain *stative passives*.)

The second difference between present participle and past participle phrases is a consequence of the first. Since they are verb phrases, both *-ing* and *-n/-ed* phrases use the five common patterns of verb complementation. However, because past participle phrases derive from passive structures, their underlying patterns are more difficult to recognize than those of present participle phrases, which are active. Though the *-n/-ed* phrase in *the man eaten at dinner* might at first glance appear to derive from pattern 1 – intransitive verb (*eaten*) + optional adverbial (*at dinner*, a prepositional phrase) – its underlying active structure is actually *Someone or something ate the man at dinner*, which follows pattern 3 (transitive verb + direct object). To discern the underlying structure of a past participle phrase, one must first make it active.

The third and final distinction between present participle and past participle phrases concerns their function. Whereas *-ing* phrases often act as nominals, *-n/-ed* phrases do not. Present participles like *walking* and *smiling* typically describe ongoing or habitual actions – they are related to the verb's *progressive aspect* – and, if we want to make such actions the subject of a discussion, it makes sense to convert them into something noun-like. By contrast, past participles such as *thrown* and *announced* describe completed actions; they are related to the verb's *perfective aspect*. It is not natural to use such words to describe activities, precisely because the action being described is no longer ongoing or "active." However, whereas *-ing* and *-n/-ed* phrases differ in being used (or not used) as nominal phrases, both occur frequently as adjectivals and infrequently as adverbials.

Like present participle phrases, past participle phrases with adjectival function usually occur in one of three positions: pre-modifying; post-modifying; and external. One-worded past participle phrases are typically pre-modifiers (*the broken win-dow*), while longer ones are shifted to post-modifying position (*the window broken in the storm*). Past participle phrases can also be shifted to a position immediately preceding the structure they modify: *Broken in the storm, the window let in great gusts of wind.*

Distingiushing past participle phrases from finite verb phrases

Since past participle phrases are non-finite verb phrases, they will never have AUX. To distinguish past participle phrases from main verbs in the passive voice, look for a form of *be* immediately preceding the past participle (which must be present in a finite verb but cannot occur in a non-finite past participle phrase). Similarly, to distinguish past participle phrases from perfective main verbs, look for the perfective aspect marker (*have*).

Passive infinitives

Infinitives can undergo the passive transformation as well, becoming PASSIVE INFINITIVES. These can function adjectivally (*the mission to be completed*) or adverbially (*To be crowned, checker pieces must reach the opponent's back row*).

A note on usage

When present participle or past participle phrases in external position are separated from the noun phrase or nominal they modify, or when the latter is omitted, the result is a DANGLING PARTICIPLE. In the sentence *Exhausted from the race, the finish line seemed miles away to the runners*, the past participle phrase *exhausted from the race* presumably refers to *the runners*, but its placement misleadingly suggests that it modifies *the finish line*. To avoid ambiguity, one might write *Exhausted from the race, the runners thought the finish line seemed miles away*. Similarly, in *Eating ravenously, the cookies disappeared quickly*, the structure being modified by *eating ravenously* has been omitted; as currently worded, the cookies are eating rather than being eaten. A version of the sentence without dangling participle might read *Eating ravenously, we made the cookies disappear quickly*.

Terms, Questions, and Exercises

PAST PARTICIPLE PHRASE, PASSIVE INFINITIVE, DANGLING PARTICIPLE.

1. What are three differences between past participle and present participle phrases?

2. Identify the non-finite past participle phrases in the sentences below and specify which function (nominal, adjectival, or adverbial) the phrase plays.

   a) You will find him famished.

   b) Writers inspired by Tolkien rarely equal his skill in world-building.

   c) The house demolished on Tuesday stood next door to a mansion.

3. What is a dangling participle? Identify any dangling participles in the sentences below:

   a) Driven to action, we see Oedipus attempt to take charge.

   b) Awed by the discovery, the audience applauded the findings.

   c) Closed at unpredictable times, I find the store frustrating.

4. Make up three passive infinitive phrases.

5. [Challenge.] Below are the first paragraphs of Abraham Lincoln's Gettysburg address (1863). Identify the past participles in the passage, then note whether they function as a part of an *active finite verb phrase*, as part of a *passive finite verb phrase*, or as part of a *non-finite past participle phrase*. Remember that a past participle in an active finite verb phrase will be preceded by a form of *have*, whereas one in a passive finite verb phrase will be preceded by a form of *be*; non-finite past participles function adjectivally or adverbially. (Example: *conceived* is part of a non-finite verb phrase, *conceived in liberty*, an adjectival which modifies *nation*.)

Four score and seven years ago, our fathers brought forth upon this continent a new nation, conceived in liberty and dedicated to the proposition that all men are created equal. (adjectival)

Now we are engaged in a great civil war (stative passive) *testing whether that nation – or any nation so conceived and so dedicated* (adj) *– can long endure. We are met on a great battlefield of* (stative passive) *that war. We have come* (active) *to dedicate a portion of it as a final resting place for those who died here that the nation might live. This we may in all propriety do. But, in a larger sense, we can not dedicate, we can not consecrate, we can not hallow this ground. The brave men, living and dead,* (adj) *who struggled here have hallowed it* (active) *far above our poor power to add or detract. The world will little note nor long remember what we say here, while it can never forget what they did here.*

19. Part 2 Review

Chapter 10 Terms
PHRASE, CONSTITUENT, HEAD, MODIFIER, PRE-MODIFIER, POST-MODIFIER, COMPLEMENT, LICENSE, PHRASE STRUCTURE TREE.

Chapter 11 Terms
ADJECTIVE PHRASE, ADVERB PHRASE, PREPOSITIONAL PHRASE.

Chapter 12 Terms
NOUN PHRASE, PRE-DETERMINER, SUBJECT-VERB AGREEMENT.

Chapter 13 Terms
VERB PHRASE, STRUCTURE OF VERB PHRASE, TIME, TENSE, SIMPLE TENSES (PRESENT, PAST), COMPOUND TENSES, PERFECTIVE ASPECT, PROGRESSIVE ASPECT, FORMULA FOR PRODUCING VERBS, LITERARY PRESENT.

Chapter 14 Terms
SUBJECT, PREDICATE, TAG QUESTION, LINKING (COPULAR) VERB, SUBJECT COMPLEMENT, PREDICATE NOMINATIVE, PREDICATE ADJECTIVE, TRANSITIVE VERB, DIRECT OBJECT, INTRANSITIVE VERB, DIRECT OBJECT COMPLEMENT, INDIRECT OBJECT, MONOTRANSITIVE VERB, DITRANSITIVE VERB, COMPLEX TRANSITIVE VERB.

Chapter 15 Terms
NON-FINITE VERB PHRASE, PRESENT PARTICIPLE PHRASE,

GERUND.

Chapter 16 Terms
BARE INFINITIVE, TO-INFINITIVE PHRASE, TO-INFINITIVE CLAUSE, SPLIT INFINITIVE.

Chapter 17 Terms
PASSIVE VOICE, ACTIVE VOICE, PASSIVE VERB MARKER, PASSIVE TRANSFORMATION, STATIVE PASSIVE, PASSIVE "GET", HEDGING.

Chapter 18 Terms
PAST PARTICIPLE PHRASE, PASSIVE INFINITIVE, DANGLING PARTICIPLE.

1. Pre-modifiers, heads, complements, and post-modifiers are components common to _____ .

2. What is a complement? Do all phrases have them? Give four examples of complements. How do you know they are complements, not modifiers?

3. What are the three positions in which adjective phrases occur?

4. What grammatical role do adverb phrases typically play? Can adverb phrases ever be complements?

5. True or false? Prepositional phrases are headed by nouns because, as object of the preposition, the noun is the most important part of the prepositional phrase.

6. Fill in the blanks:

Noun phrase

_____ _____ _____ _____ _____ _____

7. Fill in the blanks:

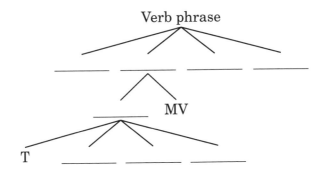

8. What's the difference between time and tense? How can you tell the difference between simple and compound tenses?

9. True or false? Present participles and past participles always convey tense – present and past tense, respectively.

10. In the blank spaces of the chart below, provide an example of each type of verb phrase complementation pattern. (Use finite verb phrases.)

　　1. Intransitive (no complement) *Ex: She ... groaned.*

　　2. Linking

　　　　a. nominal comp. – *She ...*

　　　　b. adjectival comp. – *She ...*

　　　　c. adverbial comp. – *She ...*

　　3. Monotransitive, direct obj. only – *She ...*

　　4. Ditransitive, indirect and dir. obj. – *She ...*

　　5. Complex trans., direct obj. and obj. comp.

　　　　a. nominal + nominal – *She ...*

　　　　b. nominal + adjectival – *She ...*

　　　　c. nominal + adverbial – *She ...*

11. Take three of the verb phrases you provided in the previous exercise and turn each into a present participle phrase, a to-infinitive phrase, and a bare infinitive phrase. (Example: *groaned* — *groaning*, *to groan*, and *groan*.)

12. What is the distinguishing characteristic of non-finite verb phrases?

13. Present participle phrases most often function as _____ or as _____.

14. What is a to-infinitive clause? How does it differ from a to-infinitive phrase? Give an example.

15. Name the three steps of the passive transformation.

16. Fill in the blanks:

$$T \longrightarrow (M) \rightarrow (Prf: \underline{\quad}) \rightarrow (Prg: \underline{\quad}) \rightarrow (Pas: \underline{\quad}) \rightarrow MV$$
$$\underline{\quad} \quad \underline{\quad} \qquad + \underline{\quad} \qquad + \underline{\quad} \qquad + \underline{\quad}$$

17. True or false? Past participle phrases don't often function as nominals.

18. Give an example of a passive to-infinitive.

19. Name the eight forms of the verb *be*.

20. What is "hedging"? How can the passive voice be used in hedging?

21. In each of the sentences below, identify one example of each of the five kinds of phrases (NP, VP, AdjP, AdvP, PP).

   a) The roguish actor playing Ariel winked covertly to the audience.

   b) It took a very desperate ploy to convince him of my sincerity.

c) Rushed through each part of the famous site, the tourists unfortunately did not enjoy their visit to Olympia.

22. For each of the sentences in the previous exercise, list and identify by kind one non-finite verb phrase.

23. Identify the tenses of the following verb phrases:

a) I had been working.

b) I have worked.

c) I will be working.

24. In the sentences below, identify any passive verbs:

a) The movie was shown to select audiences prior to its release.

b) Three Milky Way suns have gone supernova in the last thousand years.

c) According to Greek myth, Zeus's thunderbolt was forged by the cyclops.

25. Make the following active sentences passive. If a sentence cannot be made passive, write "N/A."

a) The lunar lander fired two retro-rockets.

b) Thor threw the hammer Mjölnir at the giant.

c) My friend Sara walked to the store yesterday.

Part III.

Clauses

20. Types of Clauses

Language is fundamentally *modular*: words combine into phrases, phrases into clauses, and clauses into sentences. Accordingly, our study of grammar has progressed from categorizing *words* according to their behavior (in Part 1) to examining how *phrases* are formed (in Part 2). The third and final section will examine *clauses*, structures that contain both a *subject* and *predicate* (though one or the other may be implied). Some of the material we will be discussing has already been introduced in chapter 8, which gave an overview of coordination, subordination, and the three kinds of subordinate clauses (nominal, adjectival, and adverbial). In the coming chapters, we will discuss these and other related topics in much greater detail.

We will begin by examining different kinds of independent clauses. The sentences studied so far have contained only DECLARATIVE CLAUSES, which use a *subject* + *predicate* pattern and most often make *statements*. They are the most common kinds of clauses. The other kinds of independent clauses are *imperative*, *interrogative*, and *exclamatory*.

As we have seen, grammatical analysis often requires making a distinction between an expression's *form* and its *function*; for instance, a string of words can be a verb phrase in form but a nominal in function. A distinction between form and function is also helpful in studying kinds of independent clauses. A clause can follow the declarative pattern but have the purpose of giving a command, posing a question, or making an exclamation. Therefore, when discussing "kinds of clauses," we will be categorizing them by their different *forms*: (*declarative*, *imperative*, *interrogative*, and *exclamatory*). Terms that describe a clause's *function* – regardless of its form – include statement, command, question, and exclamation. In analyzing kinds of independent clauses, it is important to remember this distinction.

Declarative clauses

Declarative clauses are the most common types of clauses. They employ the familiar *subject + predicate* pattern, and they can be used to formulate statements, commands, questions, and exclamations. For instance, *You're leaving now* contains a subject (*You*) and a predicate (*are leaving now*), with the predicate containing a verb and an adverb. This clause is declarative in form.

The function of the expression, however, could vary. As a statement of fact, it means something like "You're about to leave." If intended as a command, it would have the force of an order: "Get out!" One could also use it to ask a question, "Is it true that you're about to leave?" Finally, the statement could be an exclamation expressing strong emotion, as in "I can't believe that you are leaving now!"

Regardless of how it is being used in context, the form of *You're leaving now* is declarative because it employs the straightforward *subject + predicate* structure.

Imperative clauses

IMPERATIVE CLAUSES use the bare infinitive as main verb and normally have an implied subject. Theyare typically used to give directives (orders or instructions).

Again, we must distinguish between form and function. *You're leaving now* could be intended as a command, but it is not imperative in form. The imperative equivalent of *You're leaving now* would be *Leave now!* To arrive at this form, we cut

AUX from the verb – leaving the main verb's bare infinitive – and move it to sentence-initial position, then drop the subject.

To confirm that the verb must be in bare infinitive form, consider that declarative *You are quiet* becomes imperative *Be quiet*. Here, *be* serves as main verb, not an auxiliary. Just like non-finite verb phrases, imperatives do not permit auxiliary verbs: **Might be quiet! *Are being quiet!* Although the clause's subject is usually deleted, it can be retained for emphasis: *You be quiet!*

There are two special kinds of imperative. The first is the *let-imperative*, as in *Let's go to the movie, Let's be friends*, or *Let us pray*. Here the underlying meaning of *let* is "allow," "permit," which appears in expressions like *He let us have the day off*. *Let's go to the movie* could be paraphrased, *(You) allow us to go to the movie*. This is a polite way of phrasing a request or invitation. The same thing is true of *Let us pray*, which sounds less harsh than the unvarnished command, *Pray!* LET-IMPERATIVES contain two bare infinitives, *let* itself and a second verb (*go, be, pray*); *let* introduces the request, while the second verb specifies its nature (to go to the movie, to be friends, or to pray).

The second type of special imperative is the *do-imperative*. As discussed in chapter 5, *do* is one of three primary verbs, along with *have* and *be*; primary verbs can function as either main or auxiliary verbs. One of the functions of *do* is to lend emphasis to a predicate it precedes: *I do enjoy eating Chinese food, They did violate the treaty, The course of true love never did run smooth*. The DO-IMPERATIVE is simply the use of emphatic *do* in an imperative clause, as in *Do come in* or *Do sit down*.

Interrogative clauses

There are two kinds of interrogative clauses, open and closed. OPEN INTERROGATIVE CLAUSES begin with an interrogative word (*when, where, why, who / whom / whose, what, which*, or *how*) and elicit feedback that is typically not limited to a set number of choices: *Why was she late? Where did they go? Whose backpack is this?* CLOSED INTERROGATIVE CLAUSES begin with a helping verb and permit only a small number of replies: *Did the Colts, the Texans, the Jaguars, or the Titans win the AFC South?* A common type of closed interrogative is the *yes-no question*, such as *Did you enjoy your meal?*

Open and closed questions differ in structure. A declarative clause that contains a helping verb, like *You are eating a sandwich*, can be turned into a closed interrogative clause by simply moving the helping verb to clause-initial position: *Are you eating a sandwich?*

You are eating a sandwich —→ Are you __ eating a sandwich?

The __ marks the empty position resulting from the movement or deletion of a word (here, the helping verb *are*); this empty position is called a GAP. In a closed interrogative clause with several helping verbs, only the first is moved to the beginning: *You have been eating a sandwich* becomes *Have you been eating a sandwich?* not **Have been you eating a sandwich?* If no helping verb is present, the appropriate form of *do* is added and moved before the subject:

He wants to stay —→ He *does* want to stay —→

Does he __ want to stay?

To turn a closed question into a declarative clause, we simply reverse the process.

Open interrogative clauses, also known as *wh-questions*, begin with an interrogative word. Because open interrogatives give respondents more options in replying than do closed questions, their structure is also more involved. To understand why,

Someone delivered this package for us at noon.	*Who* delivered this package for us at noon?
Jon delivered *something* for us at noon.	*What* <u>did</u> Jon deliver ___ for us at noon?
Jon delivered this package *for someone* at noon.	*For whom* <u>did</u> Jon deliver this package ___ at noon?
Jon delivered this package for us *sometime*.	*When* <u>did</u> Jon deliver this package for us ___ ?

Table 20.1.: Formation of open interrogative clauses

we can examine a sample declarative clause, *Jon delivered this package for us at noon*, and some open-ended questions one could ask about the clause, including *Who delivered this package for us at noon? What did Jon deliver for us at noon? For whom did Jon deliver this package at noon? When did the Jon deliver this package for us?* These questions are suggested by the information contained in the sentence, which has a subject (*Jon*) and a predicate composed of a verb (*delivered*), a direct object (*the package*), an indirect object (*for us*), and an adverbial of time (*at noon*). If these were real questions, we would probably not know their answers, so we could also use indefinite pronouns – *someone*, *something*, and so on – to model the process whereby a declarative clause becomes an open question.

This process has three steps: first, substitute the appropriate interrogative word; second, if the interrogative is not in clause-initial position and there is no auxiliary, add *do* (as in closed questions); and third, if the question word does not already begin the clause, move it and the first auxiliary there. This may sound complicated, but native speakers of English do this without even thinking about it. Table 20.1 illustrates the process, substituting indefinite pronouns to make the relationships more obvious.

Two points remain to be addressed. Consider the following

open questions: *Which exit should we take? What dress will you wear? At whose suggestion did he quit?* The equivalent declarative sentences would be *We should take some exit, You will wear some dress,* and *He quit at someone's suggestion.* However, the above rule for forming open interrogative clauses would result in **Which should we take exit? *What will you wear dress? *Whose did he quit at suggestion?* How can we account for – and correct – these incorrectly formed questions? Note that all three examples involve question words acting as determiners: *Which exit? What dress? At whose suggestion?* (Compare *this exit, Julie's dress,* and *at my suggestion.*) When this is the case, we must move not just the question word, but also noun phrase or nominal to which the determiner belongs, to clause-initial position; if this is the object of a preposition, it is often moved as well: <u>*Which exit*</u> *should we take?* <u>*What dress*</u> *will you wear?* <u>*At whose suggestion*</u> *did he quit?*

Finally, note that in informal usage, open questions are sometimes followed by a tag that mimics the choices presented by a closed question: *Where are you going, to the office? Which direction should we head, north or south?* Don't let such constructions confuse you; they are still open questions. If in doubt, you can always distinguish open and closed questions by checking for a *wh-* word near the beginning of the interrogative clause. Open questions have one, closed questions do not.

Exclamatory clauses

Sentences that express strong emotion are not necessarily exclamatory. The following are *not* exclamatory clauses: *You must be hungry! Close the door! When did you arrive?!* The first sentence is declarative, the second imperative, and the third interrogative. These sentences may have the *function* of expressing strong emotion, but they do not have the *form* of an exclamatory clause.

EXCLAMATORY CLAUSES emphasize a particular constituent by prefacing it with *how* or *what* and moving it to initial position. *That showed courage* becomes *What courage that showed!* Likewise, *This mural is colorful* becomes *How colorful this mural is!* Unlike open interrogative clauses, which can also begin with *what* or *how* (*What/How are you doing?*), exclamatory clauses do not shift an auxiliary. Like imperatives, exclamatory clauses often omit information, as in *What courage!*

A note on usage

In open questions, if the requested information is the object of a prepositional phrase, moving the preposition is optional. If the preposition is not moved, it is separated from its object and therefore (as we learned in chapter 6) *stranded*. Compare the alternate interrogative versions of the *He quit at someone's suggestion*, where *someone's suggestion* is the object of *at*: *Whose suggestion did he quit at? At whose suggestion did he quit?* In the first version, *at* remains in place while *someone's/whose suggestion* is moved; the preposition is stranded. In the second version, the whole prepositional phrase (*at someone's/whose suggestion*) is moved, and the preposition still directly precedes its object.

Some style guides discourage ending a sentence with a preposition. This is because stranded prepositions often sound colloquial. In conversation, we would probably say, *What did you learn about?* In writing, the preferred version would be, *About what did you learn?* Likewise, *the question which I was interested in* is more colloquial than *the question in which I was interested*. In formal written English, it's usually a good idea to avoid stranded prepositions, except in cases like *What are you looking at?*, where the non-stranded alternative – *At what are you looking?* – sounds stilted.

In short, use your judgment in deciding where to place the preposition in an open question.

Terms, Questions, and Exercises

DECLARATIVE CLAUSE, IMPERATIVE CLAUSE, LET-IMPERA-
TIVE, DO-IMPERATIVE, OPEN INTERROGATIVE CLAUSE,
CLOSED INTERROGATIVE CLAUSE, GAP, EXCLAMATORY
CLAUSE.

1. What is the difference between a sentence that asks a question and an *interrogative clause*? Give an example of a question that does not use the interrogative form.

2. Write three *let-imperatives* and three *do-imperatives*.

3. What are some differences between *closed* and *open* interrogative clauses? Write a closed and an open interrogative clause for each of the following sentences:

   a) Hannah is tired because she didn't sleep enough.

   b) Drew turned the corner quickly.

   c) They left the play at the intermission.

4. Identify the kind of clause (declarative, imperative, closed interrogative, open interrogative, exclamatory) in the following sentences:

   a) What a charmer he is!

   b) You're going paint the room yellow?

   c) Has the plan changed?

   d) When did she arrive?

21. Coordination and Negation

In chapter 8, we studied the different types of conjunctions, including coordinating conjunctions (the FANBOYS) and subordinating conjunctions, as well as the kinds of structures they link. In the next several chapters, we will take a closer look at *coordination* and *subordination*, the syntactic processes whereby these links are formed. We begin by examining CO-ORDINATION, which combines two or more constituents of the same kind into a single structure and assigns equal weight to each.

Coordination

Coordinating conjunctions are used to combine constituents with similar grammatical function into a COORDINATE STRUCTURE. Constituents linked in this way are called CONJUNCTS. (Thus, two or more *conjuncts* make up a single *coordinate structure*.) As we saw in chapter 8, the FANBOYS are not all created alike. The most common and versatile ones – *and*, *but*, and *or* – can join virtually any two structures of the same type. *Nor* can do so as well, but it usually requires a preceding *neither* or *not*. *Yet* can combine adjectival and adverbial phrases, as well as clauses; *for* and *so*, only clauses.

Coordinating conjunctions combine structures of the same kind: *The zombie lurched toward me, so I fled* (coordinate clauses); *the shotgun or the rifle* (coordinate noun phrases); *The horde seemed mindless yet malignant* (coordinate adjective phrases). Joining unrelated structures does not work: *The zombie luched toward me, so the shotgun* (clause and noun phrase); *the rifle yet malignant* (noun phrase and adjective phrase); *I fled or mindless* (clause and adjective phrase). Specifically, conjuncts must have the same *grammatical function*; however, they do not necessarily have to have the same *form*. For instance, in *The survivors were tired but moving rapidly*, the coordinate structure consists of an adjective phrase (*tired*) and a verb phrase with adjectival function (*moving rapidly*); both describe *the survivors*. In *He is a marksman and accurate with any rifle*, *and* can join a noun phrase and an adjective phrase because together they function as a coordinate *subject complement* (*a marksman* is a predicate nominative, *accurate with any rifle* a predicate adjective). Again, the key attribute for two conjuncts is that they share the same grammatical function.

When analyzing the role a coordinate structure plays within a sentence, we assign the entire structure to one particular function. For instance, in *Exercise and nutrition contribute to a healthy lifestyle*, two noun phrases – *exercise* and *nutrition* – act as coordinate subject. Clauses are composed of a subject and a predicate, not a predicate and two (or three, or six) subjects. Likewise, in *She saw Mars, Jupiter, and Saturn*, the conjuncts *Mars, Jupiter*, and *Saturn* together form a single coordinate direct object; the patterns of verb phrase complementation do not allow for a verb to take three direct objects.

The fact that coordinate structures fulfill a single role but are composed of two or more conjuncts reinforces one of the most important principles of language, namely that complex structures consist of simpler ones. We have already seen this in how morphemes combine to form words, words combine to form phrases, and phrases combine to form clauses. Coordinating conjunctions extend this principle by allowing us to combine two or more structures of the same kind, an elegant example of a principle discussed in chapter 1, language's *infinite use of finite means*. Thinking only about phrases, for instance, conjunctions allow the basic phrase pattern of *pre-modifier – head – complement – post-modifier* to become far more complex and varied, making it possible to create structures like *pre-modifier BUT pre-modifier – head – complement OR complement OR complement – post-modifer AND post-modifier* (*I want you to quickly but accurately throw your grenade, her grenade, or his grenade over the wall and at the zombies*). Coordinating conjunctions can also join together entire clauses, which makes them especially versatile. The beauty of forming such intricate structures out of more basic ones is that we don't need to keep track of hundreds of different possible patterns. We only need to know a few basic ones and some rules for how these can be combined and transformed.

Note that conjunctions can be omitted, especially for rhetorical effect. Julius Caesar's *I came, I saw, I conquered* is a famous example. By omitting the *and*, the sentence emphasizes the speed and inevitability of Caesar's triumph: coming, seeing, and conquering follow one another at break-neck pace. (The effect is even more pronounced in the original Latin: *Veni, vidi, vici.*) Imagine this sentence rewritten with a heavy use of conjunctions: *After I came, I not only saw but I also conquered.* As a rule of thumb, removing conjunctions speeds up the pace of a sentence. Conversely, adding extra conjunctions slows it down. This can convey monotony (*We walked and walked and walked and walked*) or thoroughness (*There was water and milk and juice and soda and coffee and tea*).

Negation

As we learned in the previous chapter, *do* can be used as helping verb for emphasis (*I do want ice cream!*) and in forming questions (*Do you know the way?*). A third use of auxiliary *do* concerns the negation of verb phrases: *I do not think so.*

NEGATION entails reversing the polarity of an affirmative statement. Specifically, phrases and clauses can be negated through *determiners*, *adverbs*, or *conjunctions*. Noun phrases are typically negated through determiners like *no* or *neither* (*No cat enjoys swimming, Neither dog enjoys swimming*), while other kinds of phrases – as well as determiners or pre-determiners – are negated by adverbs such as *not* and *never* (*Not all the statements he made can be believed, I never lie*). Verb phrases that do not include a helping verb add *do* before the main verb when negated: *Erin ran* becomes *Erin did not run*. The indefinite pronouns beginning with *no-* (*nobody, none, noone, nothing, nowhere*) have negative meaning.

A note on usage

In chapter 8, we learned how to punctuate coordinate clauses. To review, commas – not periods or semi-colons – are used before a coordinating conjunction that joins two clauses: *Hannah took a long time to finish, but Beth was done more quickly*, not **Hannah took a long time to finish; but, Beth was done more quickly*. The comma can be omitted if the clauses are very short.

When punctuating coordinate *phrases*, do *not* use commas to separate *two* phrases joined by a conjunction (**The laptop, and the iPad were on the table*). *Do* use commas to separate *three or more* phrases. Although there is some debate over whether a comma is required before the final item in a series (the "Oxford comma" or SERIAL COMMA), American English style guides overwhelmingly recommend it. *The laptop, the iPad, and the phone were on the table* illustrates proper use of the serial comma.

Terms, Questions, and Exercises

COORDINATION, COORDINATE STRUCTURES, CONJUNCTS, NEGATION, SERIAL COMMA.

1. What is a conjunct? What kinds of structures can become conjuncts?

2. Write a sample sentence for each of the following:

   a) A sentence that has a coordinate subject consisting of two NPs.

   b) A sentence that has a coordinate direct object consisting of three NPs.

   c) A sentence that has a coordinate pre-modifier consisting of two AdjPs.

   d) A sentence that has a coordinate predicate consisting of two finite VPs.

3. What is the rule for punctuating items in a series?

4. Correct the punctuation of the sentences below:

   a) I tried to call you; but, I only got a busy signal.

   b) Several companies have created flying cars so the concept is not as far-fetched as one might assume.

   c) He added ham, and onions to the salad.

   d) She had degrees from Hanover, Vanderbilt and the University of Illinois.

22. Content Clauses

Whereas coordinating conjunctions give equal weight to the elements they join, subordinating conjunctions attach a *subordinate* (or *dependent*) clause to an independent clause; the independent clause in which a dependent clause is embedded is a MATRIX CLAUSE. Typically, subordinating conjunctions (or *subordinators*) signal the beginning of a subordinate clause: *I know that she is famous*, *The hiker who reached the summit paused*. In a few constructions, however, a subordinating conjunction can be omitted (*I know __ she is famous*).

There are three types of subordinate clauses: *nominal* subordinate clauses, which are created with content clauses; *adjectival* subordinate clauses, which are headed by relative pronouns; and *adverbial* subordinate clauses, which are headed by adverbial subordinators. In this chapter, we will take a closer look at CONTENT CLAUSES, dependent clauses formed from three of the structures examined in chapter 20 (declarative clauses, interrogative clauses, and exclamatory clauses). Adjectival and adverbial subordinate clauses will be discussed in chapters 23 and 24.

Declarative content clauses

SUBORDINATE DECLARATIVE CONTENT CLAUSES add the subordinator *that* to the beginning of a declarative clause; the resulting structure is a nominal that can fulfill most noun phrase functions. Starting with an expression like *She has written a best-selling thriller*, we simply add *that* to turn the whole into a nominal, which can now become a subject (*That she has written a best-selling thriller* is cause for celebration), a direct object (*I see that she has written a best-selling thriller*), a subject complement (*The point is that she has written a best-selling thriller*), a noun complement (*The idea that she has written a best-selling thriller pleases her friends*), or an adjective complement (*I am sure that she has written a best-selling thriller*).

As mentioned above, in some cases the *that* can be omitted: *I see ___ she has written a best-selling thriller, I am sure ___ she has written a best-selling thriller*. If in analyzing a sentence you suspect that a dependent clause has had its subordinator deleted, you can always try re-inserting one. *I forgot you are from Alaska* can become *I forgot that you are from Alaska*, which confirms that here *you are from Alaska* is a subordinate clause. *I forgot my hat* cannot take an added subordinator: **I forgot that my hat*. Thus, *my hat* is not a subordinate clause (it is a noun phrase).

Interrogative content clauses

SUBORDINATE INTERROGATIVE CONTENT CLAUSES differ from independent interrogative clauses in two ways: semantically, they *report* questions but do not directly *ask* them; and, syntactically, there is no movement of the auxiliary verb or insertion of *do* if no helping verb is present.

CLOSED INTERROGATIVE CONTENT CLAUSES add *whether* or *if* before the subject of the clause: *I wonder if the cat is hungry, They questioned whether the decision was correct*. Here the questions – *if the cat is hungry, whether the decision is correct* – are *reported* (or *indirect*). Both could be expressed directly in independent clauses: *Is the cat hungry? Is the decision correct?* The subordinators *whether* and *if* allow us to report a question without directly asking it.

OPEN INTERROGATIVE CONTENT CLAUSES differ from independent open question clauses in lacking the movement and/or insertion of an auxiliary. They already begin with an interrogative word or phrase, so they do not add any subordinators. Thus, the independent open question clause *Where is the popcorn?* has as its subordinate counterpart *I know where the popcorn is*, not **I know where is the popcorn*.

Exclamatory content clauses

SUBORDINATE EXCLAMATORY CONTENT CLAUSES are identical in form to their independent counterparts; if the clause is embedded in a matrix clause and functions as a nominal, it is subordinate. *What a genius he is* is independent if it stands alone, but in the sentence *I see what a genius he is*, it is dependent.

The function of content clauses

The subordinate clauses examined in this chapter are all nominals, even when they complement nouns or adjectives. (Adjective complements can be noun phrases, as in *It is worth the wait*.) To see why this is so, let us take a closer look at one of the examples cited above, *The idea that she has written a best-selling thriller pleases her friends*. Here, the noun *idea* has as complement the declarative content clause *that she has written a best-selling thriller*. Because it follows a noun, this subordinate clause might seem like an adjectival, but it is not. It is a complement for *the idea*. On its own, *The idea pleases her friends* is incomplete; somewhere, we must specify what *the idea* is: *that she has written a best-selling thriller*. Many nouns routinely take *that*-clauses as complements, the most common ones being *belief, fact, hope, idea, notion,* and *reason*.

A note on usage

Some authorities advise against using content clauses as noun phrase complements. In their venerable *Elements of Style*, William Strunk and E. B. White write that "the expression *the fact that* should be revised out of every sentence in which it occurs." Similar constructions include *the notion that, the idea that, the question (of) whether*, and so on. Strunk and White's declaration of war against *the fact that* comes in a chapter entitled "Omit Needless Words," and it's true that many sentences containing *the fact that* could be rewritten with little loss of meaning. However, in cases where a writer wishes to emphasize that something has been established as true or self-evident, *the fact that* can serve a useful purpose. For instance, while *The fact that you ate the last cookie bothers me* (10 words) could become *That you ate the last cookie bothers me* (8 words), the first sentence makes a stronger claim than the second. If this is the writer's intent, then the two extra words – *the fact* – are well spent.

Terms, Questions, and Exercises

MATRIX CLAUSE, CONTENT CLAUSE, SUBORDINATE DECLARA- TIVE CONTENT CLAUSE, SUBORDINATE INTERROGATIVE CON- TENT CLAUSE, CLOSED INTERROGATIVE CONTENT CLAUSE, OPEN INTERROGATIVE CONTENT CLAUSE, SUBORDINATE EX- CLAMATORY CONTENT CLAUSE.

1. What is a "content" subordinate clause?

2. How are declarative content clauses formed? Write three sentences in which *I like chocolate* is used as a declara- tive content clause, including one sentence in which the subordinator is omitted.

3. Create a subordinate interrogative content clauses from each of the following questions:

   a) Is she outside?

   b) Do you like green eggs and ham?

   c) Whose thumb drive was left behind?

4. What is the difference between independent and dependent exclamatory clauses?

5. How can we distinguish a subordinate clause with omitted subordinator from an independent clause?

6. Identify the independent and the subordinate clauses in the following sentences:

   a) They had no lead on who robbed the museum.

   b) The inspector wondered why the alarm did not go off.

   c) That the suspect had a key became clear later.

7. In the sentence *The notion that life continues after death is one of the oldest human beliefs*, should *the notion* be omitted? Why or why not?

23. Relative Clauses

RELATIVE CLAUSES are dependent clauses headed by a relative subordinator (*which*, *that*, *who*, *whose*, and *whom*); they always function as adjectivals.

Structure and function of relative clauses

Relative clauses combine two independent clauses with the same topic into a single sentence, with one clause becoming subordinate: *He wanted a book* and *The book was expensive* can become *He wanted a book that was expensive* or *The book that he wanted was expensive.*

To see how relative clauses are formed, we can imagine the following process taking place. First, the clause that will be subordinated is dropped inside the matrix clause, after the noun being modified: *The book [He wanted a book] was expensive.* Next, an appropriate subordinator — like *that* — is substituted for the duplicate structure: *The book* [He wanted a ~~book~~ that] *was expensive.* Finally, the subordinator is moved to the beginning of the subordinate clause: *The book [that he wanted] was expensive.*

As with open interrogative clauses, the possessive subordinator *whose* will "bring along" the noun phrase it modifies, and, if the relative clause is the object of a preposition, that preposition is often moved as well. For instance, following the three-step process described above, the sentences *We ate at a restaurant* and *The restaurant was crowded* can be combined as follows: 1. *The restaurant [We ate at a restaurant] was crowded*; 2. *The restaurant [we ate at ~~a restaurant~~ which] was crowded*; and 3. *The restaurant [at which we ate] was crowded* or, less formally, *The restaurant [which we ate at] was crowded*. Similarly, *The superhero's weakness was kryptonite* can be subordinated to *The superhero stumbled*: 1. *The superhero [the superhero's weakness was kryptonite] stumbled*; 2. *The superhero [the superhero's whose weakness was kryptonite] stumbled*; and 3. *The superhero [whose weakness weakness was kryptonite] stumbled*.

In some cases, the relative subordinator can be omitted, which can be indicated with __: *The book __ he wanted was expensive*. Notionally, the subordinator is still present; if it weren't, the relative clause would incomplete: **He wanted* lacks its direct object, *the book*.

Who versus *whom*

Deciding on the correct usage of *whom* gives almost everyone trouble. In informal usage, *whom* has become extinct, but it is alive and well in formal written English.

Who and *whom* are subject and object forms of the relative subordinator. It may help to know that the *-m* in *whom* derives from an Old English inflectional morpheme also present in *him* and *them* (compare the subject forms *he* and *they*, which do not end in *-m*). If the subordinator acts as the subject of the relative clause, the proper form is *who*; if it acts as the object, *whom* is correct. A rule of thumb that often works is to use *whom* when *him* or *them* would also work, and *who* when *he* or *they* would be appropriate.

Let's apply this to some concrete examples. For instance, should it be *The speaker who was at a loss for words hesitated* or *The speaker whom was at a loss for words hesitated*? We begin by isolating the relative clause, *who(m) was at a loss for words*, from the matrix clause, *The speaker hesitated*. Within the relative clause, *who(m)* functions as the subject, analogous to *he*: *He was at a loss for words*. Therefore, the subject form is correct: *The speaker who was at a loss for words hesitated*. To take another example, should one write, *The senator who Terry wrote replied* or *The senator whom Terry wrote replied*? Again, we begin by separating the relative clause, *who(m) Terry wrote*, from its matrix clause (*The senator replied*). Next, we identify subject of the relative clause, answering the question *Who wrote?* Terry. Since *who(m)* is not the subject, it must function as object; we can confirm this by reverting the relative clause into its independent form and substituting *him*: *Terry wrote him (the senator)*. Thus, the object form is correct: *The senator whom Terry wrote replied*.

Distinguishing relative clauses from other subordinate clauses

Relative clauses can appear similar to open interrogative content clauses; both can be headed by *who, whom, whose,* or *which*. To keep these apart, remember that relative clauses are adjectivals that modify a noun, while open interrogative content clauses act as nominals.

In previous chapters, we've used the personal pronoun substitution test to identify structures acting like noun phrases, with a successful substitution indicating that the structure in question is nominal. Let's try this here with two sentences, *They had no lead on who robbed the museum* and *The man who robbed the museum had inside help*. In both cases, the subordinate clause is *who robbed the museum*. When we substitute a personal pronoun for this structure in both sentences, we get *They had no lead on it* (which works) and **The man he robbed the museum* (which doesn't). This confirms that, in the first sentence, *who robbed the museum* is an open interrogative clause functioning as a nominal, while in the second it is a relative clause with adjectival function, modifying man.

One wrinkle to be aware of is that the pronoun substitution

test will not work for two nominals that occur in succession, such as when one noun phrase or nominal acts as the complement of another, as in *I have no clue what you are talking about*: **I have no clue it*. We know that *what you are talking about* cannot be an adjectival because *what* is not a relative conjunction (which are *who, whom, whose, that,* and *which*). To confirm that *what you are talking about* is a complement rather than a modifier, we can try the test of omission, stacking, and rearrangement. If we remove the clause, we get *I have no clue,* which only as works as the answer to a question: *Where is he? I have no clue.* The answer implies *I have no clue about where he is.* In other words, in *I have no clue what you are talking about,* the clause *what you are talking about* provides pivotal information that can't be omitted. This confirms that it is a nominal complement, not an adjectival modifier. The test also does not work for two nominals or noun phrases *in apposition* (that is, ones referring to the same entity), as in *The plane, an Airbus A320, landed safely in the Hudson River*: **The plane, it landed safely in the Hudson River.*

A note on usage

When punctuating relative clauses, we distinguish between *restrictive* and *non-restrictive* relative clauses. RESTRICTIVE (or DEFINING) relative clauses provide information that restricts the scope of the noun they modify, usually through implicit contrast, whereas NON-RESTRICTIVE (or NON-DEFINING) relative clauses simply provide further information about the noun they modify. For instance, in *Those flowers which bloom in winter are cold-hardy, which bloom in winter* is a restrictive clause because it limits the scope of *flowers*. Which flowers are cold-hardy? Those *which bloom in winter*. This statement also implies that there are flowers which are not cold-hardy; most tropical flowers fit this description. However, if the relative clause is bracketed by commas, its meaning changes: *Those flowers, which bloom in winter, are cold-hardy*. The sentence now suggests that the flowers being referenced *all* bloom in winter and are therefore *all* cold-hardy. (For instance, we might be discussing winter crocuses, irises, and snowdrops; all of these bloom in winter.)

Terms, Questions, and Exercises

RELATIVE CLAUSE, RESTRICTIVE (DEFINING) RELATIVE CLAUSE, NON-RESTRICTIVE (NON-DEFINING RELATIVE CLAUSE).

1. List the relative subordinators. What grammatical function do relative clauses play?

2. Combine the clauses below into a single sentence by making one a relative clause.

   a) The magician waved his wand over the card. The card disappeared.

   b) The actor was Patrick Stewart. We applauded the actor.

   c) The game became an instant classic. The game's mechanic was novel.

3. What other kind of subordinate clause do relative clauses resemble? How can one tell the difference between them?

4. In the sentences below, mark the underlined subordinate clauses as "relative" or "other."

   a) Do you know <u>why dead men tell no tales</u>?

   b) The sequel, <u>for which I am waiting</u>, may close this plot-hole.

   c) [Challenge.] The fact <u>that he knows her name</u> means nothing.

d) [Challenge.] The questions <u>we want to raise</u> may prove controversial.

5. For the sentences below, identify the relative clauses. Then, categorize each as restrictive or non-restrictive.

a) The movie, which I want to see, features a young Ralph Fiennes.

b) The movie I want to see features a young Ralph Fiennes.

c) Her friends who are athletes will pass the fitness test easily.

d) Her friends, who are athletes, will pass the fitness test easily.

24. Adverbial Clauses

The third kind of subordinate clauses are adverbial clauses. ADVERBIAL SUBORDINATE CLAUSES are formed by prefacing an independent clause with an adverbial subordinator; as their name indicates, such clauses function adverbially.

Structure and function of adverbial clauses

Like declarative subordinate content clauses, which add clause-initial *that*, adverbial subordinate clauses simply join a subordinator like *after*, *although*, or *because* to the beginning of a clause: *You left* can become *after you left*, *although you left*, *because you left*, and so on.

Like adverbs, adverbial subordinate clauses commonly provide information about *time* (*when we've eaten the snacks*), place (*where there's food*), or *manner* (*as if you're still hungry*). However, subordinate clauses can also convey logical relationships such as *cause-effect* (*because there's no food, so that we can eat*), *comparison-contrast* (*just as we have snacked before, although we are hungry*), and *condition-contingency* (*once we have acquired a stash of pretzels*).

Common subordinators that introduce adverbial clauses of time include *after*, *as*, *as soon as*, *before*, *once*, *since*, and *until*; of place, *anywhere*, *where*, and *wherever*; of manner, *as*, *as if*, and *as though* (and, in informal use, *like*); of cause-effect, *as*, *because*, *since*, *so*, and *so that*; of comparison-contrast, *although*, *as*, *as if*, *just as*, *though*, *whereas*, and *while*; and of condition-contingency, *as long as, if, in case, once, provided (that)*, and *unless*.

Distinguishing adverbial clauses from other subordinate clauses

As discussed in the previous chapters, the different kinds of subordinate clauses can be distinguished by function; subordinate content clauses are *nominal*, relative clauses *adjectival*, and adverbial clauses *adverbial*.

Perhaps the easiest way to distinguish adverbial clauses is via a movement test. Like adverbs, adverbial clauses are mobile. They can almost always be moved before the matrix clause (*Once we have eaten, we will go*) or after it (*We will go once we have eaten*). Also, related single adverbs can often substitute for adverbial clauses (*then* for clauses of time and *there* for clauses of place).

Adverbial clauses can resemble open interrogative content clauses. *When* and *where* are both interrogative and adverbial subordinators, so only context can determine the function of the clauses they introduce. If the clause is adverbial, it can almost always be moved, and the adverb substitution test should work. If neither is the case, confirm that the clause is interrogative (and therefore nominal) by applying the pronoun substitution test; this will work unless the nominal is in apposition or functions as a noun or adjective complement, as in *I'm not sure when the train left* (**I'm not sure it*). If the clause looks like a nominal but does not pass the pronoun substitution test, see if it is functioning as an appositive (restating a noun phrase) or as a complement (completing the meaning of a noun or adjective).

Let's try this with two sentences, *I know when the train left* and *He sighed when the train left*. In the first sentence, the pronoun substitution test works (*I know it*), but the adverb substitution test does not (*I know then*), and the movement test produces odd syntax (*When the train left, I know*). These three facts indicate that, in the first sentence, *when the train left* is a nominal (open interrogative) clause. By contrast, in the second sentence the pronoun substitution test does not work (*He sighed it*), but the movement test (*When the train left, he sighed*) and the adverb replacement test (*He sighed then*) do. Thus, *when the train left* functions adverbially in the second sentence.

A note on usage

In chapter 8, we noted that coordinating conjunctions form tight syntactic bonds with clauses and (in formal writing) do not begin sentences, while conjunctive adverbs form loose syntactic bonds and often do begin sentences.

Adverbial subordinators resemble coordinating conjunctions in forming tight syntactic bonds with the clauses to which they are joined. Thus, there is no comma after the adverbial subordinator, and the dependent clause must be in the same sentence as its matrix clause. Therefore, the first period and the comma in the following are incorrectly placed: *Bayern controlled the game. Though, they had a player sent off.* Here, the subordinate clause (*though they had a player sent off*) is placed in a different sentence from its matrix clause (*Bayern controlled the game*), and the adverbial subordinator is incorrectly separated with a comma from the clause it introduces. When the subordinate clause comes first, we separate it from the matrix clause with a comma: *Though they had a player sent off, Bayern controlled the game.*

As noted in chapter 8, concessive adverbial clauses – which "concede" a point that seems to contradict the matrix clause – are usually separated with a comma even when they come at the *end* of a sentence: *We thought we saw a fire, though we were mistaken.*

Terms, Questions, and Exercises

ADVERBIAL SUBORDINATE CLAUSE.

1. Name kinds of information that adverbial clauses commonly convey.

2. In the sentences below, identify the adverbial clause and describe what information it conveys (time, place, manner, cause-effect, comparison-contrast, or condition-contingency):

   a) Unless you complete the puzzle in thirty seconds, the game ends.

   b) While she was recovering from a knee injury, she played a lot of Solitaire.

   c) The man walked as though he had something to hide.

3. For each of the sentences below, identify the subordinate clause. Then, categorize each as nominal, adjectival, adverbial:

   a) He doesn't remember where he left his keys.

   b) Although he suffered from asthma, Roosevelt loved the outdoors.

   c) Because he always remained calm under pressure, Björn Borg was nick-named the "Ice Man."

   d) The drama that unfolded held viewers spell-bound.

4. Correct the punctuation of the sentences below. (If they are already correctly punctuated, write "correct.")

   a) I really like full-fat yogurt. Although, it's quite caloric.

   b) Twelve publishers rejected her novel, however Rowling did not give up.

   c) They critiqued his short story. While he took notes.

25. Ellipsis and Clauses of Comparison

The grammar of a sentence can sometimes be complicated by ELLIPSIS, the omission of words or phrases that must be inferred from context. There are two kinds of ellipsis: optional and required. Optional ellipsis occurs across a wide range of grammatical structures. Required ellipsis is rarer but does occur in *clauses of comparison*.

Optional ellipsis

As noted in chapter 20, non-declarative clauses routinely omit various grammatical elements: imperative clauses usually omit the subject (*[You] Continue!*); exclamatory clauses can elide both subject and verb (*What a nice apartment [this is]!*); and interrogative clauses can entail ellipsis in either question or answer (*Who went? Terry [went]*).

Ellipsis facilitates conciseness. Without it, most coordinate structures would contain lots of repetition. Thus, the second of two identical words in coordinate structures is often omitted: *the president and [the] vice president*; *red cars and [red] trucks*; *The first plane was delayed, but the second [plane] arrived on time*; *Hannah can sing, and Mary can [sing], too*; *a list of kings and [of] queens of England*. The different components of verb phrases – helping verbs, the main verb, and complements – can each be omitted in different contexts; thus, *Superman can fly and Batman [can] reason* omits the modal, while *Superman did not defeat Lex Luthor, but Batman did [defeat Lex Luthor]* elides the main verb and complement.

Optional ellipsis is also common in subordinate clauses. As mentioned in chapter 23, relative subordinators like *which*, *whom*, and *that* can often be omitted: *the book [which] I read*; *the movie [that] we saw*; *the man [whom] we met*. Furthermore, in adverbial subordinate clauses, subjects and forms of *be* can be elided: *Though [the package was] large, the package was not heavy*; *I had an idea while [I was] meditating*.

Required ellipsis: clauses of comparison

Required ellipsis most often involves comparisons. When a comparison uses a focusing morpheme or word (*-er*, *more*, *less*, or *as*) to announce the first term being compared and follows this with a subordinating conjunction (*than* or *as*) to signal its resolution, the second term is a CLAUSE OF COMPARISON.

Typically, the omitted words occur in the second term of comparison, as for instance in *Secretariat is more famous than Man o' War [is famous]*. If the verb is a form of the verb *be*, it is often not elided: *Secretariat is more famous than Man o' War is [famous]*. If it is not, *do* can be used: *Man o' War won more races than Secretariat did [win races]*.

The ellipsis can also occur in the first term of comparison: *More juniors than seniors went to the talk* has the underlying form *More juniors went to the talk than seniors went to the talk*. Some sentences even omit words in both terms. For instance, *Though younger than Pompey, Caesar equaled his ambition* has the underlying form *Though Caesar was younger than Pompey was young, Caesar equaled his ambition*.

Comparative clauses function adverbially. For instance, in *Secretariat is more famous than Man o' War [is famous]*, *than Man o' War* describes how *famous* Secretariat is; *more famous* is the comparative form of the adjective. In *Man o' War won more races than Secretariat [won races]*, *than Secretariat* modifies the determiner *more*, which quantifies the races won by

Man o' War. Finally, in *Though [Caesar was] younger than Pompey [was young], Caesar equaled his ambition*, *than Pompey* modifies *younger*.

A note on usage

In informal contexts, speakers often omit the second term of a comparison. Advertisers do this deliberately, as in the slogan Avis Rent a Car used from 1962 to 2012: *We try harder*. In formal writing, the comparative degree of an adjective, like *harder*, requires a second term: *We try harder than the competition*. Of course, this is not as memorable as *We try harder*; the Avis slogan deliberately violates the norms of formal English to create a more catchy motto.

A comparison that switches mid-stream can cause jumbled syntax. For instance, in *Rome is as famous, or even more famous than Athens*, the omission of the second *as* makes the sentence difficult to punctuate. If the word is inserted in its proper place, the difficulty disappears: *Rome is as famous as – or even more famous than – Athens*.

Terms, Questions, and Exercises

ELLIPSIS, CLAUSE OF COMPARISON.

1. What kinds of words or phrases does ellipsis usually entail?

2. In what kinds of structures does optional ellipsis often occur? Where does required ellipsis most commonly occur?

3. Identify the omitted words in the sentences below:

   a) One's virtues and vices are often linked.

   b) I watered the first flower bed, but not the second.

c) William the Conqueror was the first Norman king of England; Stephen of Blois, the last.

4. In the following sentences, indicate any clauses of comparison and specify what elements they modify. If there are no clauses of comparison, write "None."

a) In the long run, grit is as important as talent.

b) Platinum is far rarer than gold.

c) Steve Wozniak co-founded Apple with Steve Jobs.

26. Movement, Conditionals, and the Subjunctive Mood

Like ellipsis, *movement* can complicate grammatical analysis. MOVEMENT occurs when a constituent's position is shifted. Broadly speaking, there are two types of movement: semantic and syntactic. A special kind of syntactic movement occurs when verbs employ the *subjunctive mood*.

Semantic and syntactic movement

The normal pattern of declarative clauses is *subject – predicate*, with the predicate further consisting of *pre-modifier, verb, verb complement*, and *post-modifier*. SEMANTIC MOVEMENT shifts one or more of these elements for emphasis. Frequently, a verb phrase structure is moved to clause-initial position: *Quietly she left the meeting* (compare *She quietly left the meeting*); *This ingredient I've never used before* (*I've never used this ingredient before*); *A coward he was not* (*He was not a coward*). The subject can be moved as well, typically to clause-final position; delaying the subject in this manner creates a sense of anticipation. For instance, a sentence like *Sitting in the garage under a tarp was a red 1988 Ferrari Testarossa* withholds crucial information – What was sitting in the garage? – to pique the reader's interest. This sense of anticipation is lost in a sentence that arranges all of the elements in their default order: *A red 1988 Ferrari Testarossa was sitting in the garage under a tarp.*

We have already encountered SYNTACTIC MOVEMENT – positional shifts due to a syntactic constraint – in several different contexts, including indirect object movement, the passive transformation, and the formation of non-declarative and subordinate clauses. Another kind of syntactic movement occurs in *conditionals*, wherein auxiliary movement can on occasion substitute for the normal *if* + *clause* pattern: *If he should leave* can become *Should he leave*, and *If you had been there* could also be written *Had you been there*. In addition to *should* and *had*, the other auxiliary verbs that can be moved in conditionals are *were* (*Were we to object*) and, in a few fossilized expressions, *be* (*Be they alive or dead.*) In such expressions, *were* and *be* employ the *subjunctive mood*.

The subjunctive mood

Mood, like (active or passive) *voice*, is a conventional term used to describe a verb's form. The SUBJUNCTIVE MOOD is a marked form used to describe situations that run counter to established fact, especially conditional or hypothetical statements, wishes, and commands. It contrasts with the INDICATIVE MOOD (the form used in declarative clauses) and the IMPERATIVE MOOD (which occurs in imperative clauses); as discussed in chapter 20, the *indicative* mood uses the unmarked verb forms, while the *imperative* mood uses bare infinitives. There are two subjunctive forms in modern English: the bare infinitive, used mainly in wishes and commands, which is distinguishable in forms like come *what may* (not **comes what may*), suffice *it to say*, or *We ask that they* be *spared*; and *were*, which is used primarily in conditionals, such as *if I* were *you*.

Historically, the subjunctive mood has been gradually disappearing from the English verb system. Old English had a whole set of inflectional endings for the subjunctive, which, by the late Middle English period, had given way to the few forms that still survive today. The function of the subjunctive mood has largely been taken over by modal verbs. As is the case with *whom*, the subjunctive mood is found mostly in formal written English, and native speakers are often unsure of when to use it. There is also evidence that the decline of the subjunctive is still ongoing, with subjunctive forms becoming increasingly rare even in written texts.

A note on usage

In informal usage, *was* has replaced subjunctive *were* in conditional statements contrary to fact, as in *I wish I was...* (*there, in Dixie, a millionaire, taller*, and so on). Because the expressions are counter-factual, formal English uses *were* in them: *I wish were there, I wish I were in Dixie* (with apologies to Daniel Decatur Emmett), *I wish I were a millionaire, I wish I were taller*.

Note that, when a statement is *not* contrary to fact, the indicative mood is correct: *She asked if Tom was angry* or *He said that, if the trail was too long, we could take a shorter one.* The statements underlying these hypotheticals could be true: Tom might be angry; the trail could be too long. Thus, *was* is correct in both cases.

Terms, Questions, and Exercises

MOVEMENT, SEMANTIC MOVEMENT, SYNTACTIC MOVEMENT, SUBJUNCTIVE MOOD, INDICATIVE MOOD, IMPERATIVE MOOD.

1. In the sentences below, shift one or more elements to clause-initial or clause-final position. If a sentence can be rearranged in different ways, choose one. (For example, *I did not see an eagle: An eagle I did not see.*)

   a) A fox lived in the hole.

b) I saw Cellini's "Perseus with the Head of Medusa" in Italy.

c) A map was hidden in the bottom of the trunk.

2. Give an example of auxiliary movement in conditionals. Which auxiliaries can do this?

3. For the expressions below, indicate which form of the verb is correct; briefly explain your rationale:

a) If I (was / were) you, I would think about the offer.

b) We wondered if she (was / were) studying or going for a walk.

c) The attorney asked that the hearing (is / be) adjourned.

27. Punctuation

Now that we've covered the basic principles of grammar, we will look at how they can be applied. We'll begin by taking a closer look at punctuation. Various notes on usage throughout this book have already discussed many specific rules of punctuation. With a thorough understanding of words, phrases, and clauses, we can take a broader look at the subject.

Origin and function of punctuation

in the early middle ages written texts had no commas periods hyphens or other familiar marks of punctuation all the words simply ran together on the page the reader had to figure out how to assemble these words into units of sense phrases clauses and sentences

Compare this with: *In the early Middle Ages, written texts had no commas, periods, hyphens, or other familiar marks of punctuation. All the words simply ran together on the page. The reader had to figure out how to assemble these words into units of sense – phrases, clauses, and sentences.* Which is easier to read?

Punctuation helps readers process texts more efficiently and accurately. Knowing a bit more about the origin and evolution of our modern system of punctuation may help to put this into perspective.

The earliest English texts had no commas, periods, quotation marks, capital letters, or any of the other aids for comprehension that modern readers take for granted. Recognizably modern punctuation emerged only during the Renaissance, and even then there was only a rough consensus as to how the different marks should be used. Because writing is, in essence, the spoken word transferred to the page, early grammarians modeled marks of punctuation on the different kinds of pauses used in speaking; they recommended a comma for a short pause and a period a long one.

This loose use of punctuation was the norm for centuries. For instance, the most popular handbook of grammar of the early 1800s advised students to simply break up long sentences by putting a comma before the verb, giving the example *The good taste of the present age, has not allowed us to neglect the cultivation of the English language.* Modern usage would regard this as an error, for a sentence's subject and predicate should not be separated by a comma, unless to set off a parenthetical expression (as in *The good taste of the present age, however, has not allowed us to neglect the cultivation of the English language.*) Thus, our rules of punctuation are not timeless and immutable, and they will no doubt continue to evolve.

To sum up, PUNCTUATION is the practice of inserting marks to help readers interpret written texts. Three principles govern punctuation: generally, punctuation aims to capture the rhythms of spoken language; these rhythms naturally correspond to grammatical structures; and finally, some rules are conventional, meaning that they cannot be deduced but must be learned.

Corresponding to these three principles are three methods that you can use to improve your mastery of punctuation. The easiest technique entails reading your writing aloud while paying close attention to its rhythms; this simple procedure will eliminate the vast majority of punctuation errors. However, it will only take you so far. The next step is to acquire a knowledge of grammar, including of technical terms like *coordinating conjunction* and *subordinate clause*, which you've been doing by reading this book. After that, you only need to grasp the purpose of the different marks, to remember a few rules governing their use, and then to get plenty of practice applying these. Let's get started!

Periods

The SENTENCE is the largest unit of grammar; it consists of one or more clauses, at least one of which is independent, joined into a self-contained unit. There are no hard and fast rules about how much information can go into one sentence. In practice, sentences vary in length from monosyllabic constructions to utterances that run hundreds or even thousands of words in length, like the famous thirty-six page stream-of-consciousness sentence in James Joyce's *Ulysses*. (For obvious reasons, I won't cite the sentence here.) Thus, it's best to think of the sentence as consisting of words that comprise a unit. Some writers, like Joyce, habitually craft long sentences; others, such as Ernest Hemingway, prefer short ones.

The mark of punctuation used to delineate sentences that make statements is the PERIOD. (Questions, commands, and exclamations normally use question or exclamation marks.) Periods also signal abbreviations (as in *U.S.A.* or *Dr. Healwell*). In comparison with the colon, semi-colon, and comma, the period represents the longest pause in spoken language.

Because they do convey a pause, periods have a rhetorical function as well as a syntactic one. In exploiting this rhetorical function, informal writing often ignores the stipulations that sentences should consist of self-contained units and that each sentence should include at least one independent clause. The language of advertising, in particular, abounds in constructions like *Our biggest sale ever. From now through April 1st* or *All the flavor. Half the fat.*

Note that, according to convention, relative pronouns like *which* cannot begin a sentence, even when they function as subject. Thus, in *It grew late. Which is why we left*, *Which is why we left* would not be considered a well-formed sentence. Although expressions like *Which is why we left* are syntactically well-formed in that they follow a *subject* + *predicate* structure, current rules of usage dictate that a clause beginning with a relative pronoun cannot be a self-contained unit. Thus, the correct way to punctuate the above clauses would be *It grew late, which is why we left*. This is a good example of a rule that cannot be deduced but must be learned. According to this rule, personal and demonstrative pronouns can begin a sentence, while relative pronouns cannot. Thus, *It grew late; it is why we left* and *It grew late; that is why we left* would be correct, but *It grew late; which is why we left* would not.

Colons and semi-colons

Colons and semi-colons set off units shorter than those delineated by periods and longer than those indicated by commas; in speech, they represent mid-length pauses.

A COLON is used at the end of a clause to signal that the words which follow are logically related to what has been said before; their most common use is to introduce lists (*There are three kinds of mathematicians: those who can count and those who can't*) and quotations (*Alexander Pope quipped: "Fools rush in where angels fear to tread."*) A common error is to place a colon in the middle of a clause, as in *Success depends on: talent, sweat, and luck*, or *There are three kinds of mathematicians, including: those who can count and those who can't*.

A SEMI-COLON can be used in place of a period where two ideas are closely connected, and it can be used in place of a comma to separate items in a list, especially ones that already have commas (*We visited Salt Lake City, Utah; Idaho Falls, Idaho; and Jackson Hole, Wyoming*).

Semi-colons are useful for indicating logical relationships between ideas, but sentences that contain them also tend to be longer than those without.

Commas

The COMMA denotes the briefest pause in speech. Its three primary functions are to set off words that disrupt the normal flow of a sentence, to separate items in a list, and to join independent clauses.

Interrupting structures are most often modifiers that have been moved, especially adverbials. The normal pattern of a declarative clause is *Subject + Predicate*, with the prototypical structure being NP + VP. Adverbials that modify a verb are by definition either pre-modifiers or post-modifiers, and their natural position is therefore before the verb itself or after the VP complement. Because their mobility allows adverbials to move within the clause, they can also occur in sentence-initial position, as well as after the subject. For instance, in the sentence *James felt confident because he knew the answer*, the subordinate clause *because he knew the answer* is a post-modifying adverbial describing *why* James felt confident. When it is moved, this clause is set off with commas: *Because he knew the answer, James felt confident*, or *James, because he knew the answer, felt confident*. Similarly, when a post-modifying adjectival phrase or clause is moved before its head, it is also marked off with commas: *The train leaving at noon was crowded* has no comma because *leaving at noon* is in its normal (post-modifying) position; however, in *Leaving at noon, the train was crowded* it is set off by a comma because it has been moved before its head.

Other structures, too, can be moved out of position: *Whose woods these are, I think I know*, would ordinarily read *I think I know whose woods these are* (with apologies to Robert Frost). Other kinds of interrupting elements include conjunctive adverbs (*However, we have another task to do*), interjections (*Whew, it's nice to be finished*), noun phrases in apposition (*The job, moving a dresser, would not be easy*), and non-restrictive adjective clauses (*The dresser, which was large and made of oak, was heavy*).

Commas are also used to separate three or more items in

a list, including before a coordinating conjunction, as in *apple juice, lemonade, and iced tea*; here the commas indicate phrase boundaries. Commas can be omitted between adjectives that precede a noun (*a dirty old brown shirt*), and they can also stand in for coordinating conjunctions (*a brooding, heavy cloud*).

The use of commas to join independent clauses with a coordinating conjunction was discussed in the usage note to chapter 8.

Dashes

Like commas, DASHES signal the presence of an interrupting element; paired dashes signal parenthetical material in the *middle* of a sentence, and single dashes indicate added information at the *end* of a sentence. Because dashes are visually more prominent than commas, they allow the writer to set off material more emphatically than with commas, as in *The plane finally landed at 11:30 – not at 9*. They can also be used to nest independent clauses within other clauses without a coordinating conjunction: *We considered the proposal carefully – we would have been remiss in not doing so – before rejecting it.*

Apostrophes

APOSTROPHES have three functions: they signal omitted letters or numbers (as in *can't* for *cannot* or *'68* for *1968*); they mark the possessive form of nouns (*Tolkien's, the Dursleys' house*); and they form the plural of single lowercase letters (*Dot your i's and cross your t's*). As recently as the 1980s, the majority of style guides recommended using apostrophes for the plurals of numbers (*two 747's, the 1980's*), but today opinion has shifted toward omitting them (*747s, 1980s*).

A note on usage

Comma errors account for the majority of all mistakes in punctuation. These mistakes can be divided into four categories: missing commas; extra commas; commas used in place of periods; and periods used in place of commas.

To avoid missing commas, remember to place them before the last item in a series (*coffee, tea, and juice*), around a parenthetical element (*The Matterhorn, one of the tallest mountains in Europe, was first scaled in 1865*), after an introductory phrase or clause (*As von Clausewitz noted, war is the continuation of politics by other means*), and before clauses joined by coordinating conjunctions. Concessive adverbial clauses are usually separated with a comma even when they come at the end of a sentence: *We agreed, while he did not.*

Extra commas are less common than missing ones. When they do occur, they are often found before a list (**Her favorite pets are, cats, dogs, and rabbits*) or between subject and predicate (**Argentina's University of Buenos Aires, enrolls over 700,000 students*).

When a period or semi-colon appears in place of a comma, the result is a SENTENCE FRAGMENT, a structure punctuated as a sentence but lacking an independent clause: **Lewis Carroll's "Through the Looking-Glass" appeared in 1871; six years after "The Adventures of Alice in Wonderland."*

A comma used in place of a period or semi-colon creates a COMMA SPLICE, two independent clauses joined only by a comma: **Windows is installing updates, don't turn off your computer.* Not all languages forbid comma splices; they are perfectly acceptable in French and German, for example. In English, however, independent clauses must normally be joined by a coordinating conjunction (*Windows is installing updates, so don't turn off your computer*) or separated by a period or semi-colon (*Windows is installing updates; don't turn off your computer*).

Terms, Questions, and Exercises

PUNCTUATION, SENTENCE, PERIOD, COLON, SEMI-COLON, COMMA, DASH, APOSTROPHE, SENTENCE FRAGMENT, COMMA SPLICE.

1. Name two requirements for a group of words to function as a sentence.

2. What are the three primary functions of commas?

3. Which mark of punctuation is often used to introduce items in a list and quotations?

4. In punctuating clauses, semi-colons can often be used in place of periods. When should one use a semi-colon?

5. Like commas, dashes can be used to set off interrupting elements. In what circumstance should one use a dash?

6. What are three functions of the apostrophe?

7. Using the conventions of formal written English, correct the punctuation errors in the sentences below. (If there are none, write "none.")

   a) Commonly known as Custer's Last Stand the Battle of the Little Bighorn, was part of the Great Sioux War.

   b) It pitted the combined forces of the Sioux, Arapaho and Northern Cheyenne tribes, against the U.S. 7th Cavalry Regiment.

   c) Custer estimated the size of the hostile army to be around 800 warriors. Which was less than half its probable size.

   d) Custer personally commanded five companies in the battle, all were killed to the last man.

8. Give two examples of how the rules of punctuation have continued to evolve since the early 1800s.

28. Kinds of Style

The word "style" derives from an ancient writing implement, the *stylus*, used to scratch letters on wax-covered tablets. From there, "style" evolved to mean "writing," then "how an author writes," and finally to "how someone does something." In this chapter, we will focus on the second of these meanings, that is, STYLE as a writer's characteristic use of language, and specifically on the grammatical aspects of style.

Levels of style

There are different ways to describe a writer's style. One system, widely used since classical antiquity, divides styles into three levels: the *grand* style, the *middle* style, and the *plain* style. The GRAND (HIGH) STYLE is elaborate and ornamental, aiming to please and impress readers through its sophisticated diction and figures of speech. On the other extreme, the PLAIN (LOW) STYLE communicates in the most straight-forward way possible; it employs only easily-understood words and simple syntax. The MIDDLE STYLE aims to combine the virtues of the high and low styles, being both comprehensible and enjoyable, while at the same time also avoiding the excesses of both (the grand style can be stilted and confusing, the plain style boring and repetitive).

In antiquity, each level of style was associated with a particular medium of communication: the grand style was appropriate to the most formal works of literature, like epics and tragedies; the middle style was employed in didactic works; and the low style was used in works that imitated everyday speech. The greatest authors mastered all three levels of style and could use each in the appropriate context. For instance, Virgil was esteemed for writing a great epic in the high style (*The Aeneid*), a didactic work in the middle style (*The Georgics*), and poems about rural life in the plain style (*The Eclogues*).

The tripartite division of styles into high, middle, and low remains useful because it allows us to make broad distinctions between kinds of style. Today, the contemporary equivalent of the grand style is used in literary fiction and academic writing, the plain style in advertising and informal communication, and the middle style for everything in between. Of course, these broad categories – like broad categories of all kinds – oversimplify. Not all literary fiction or academic writing uses the formal style, and, for that matter, there is considerable variation in advertising copy. Thus, in distinguishing between *formal*, *middle*, and *informal* registers of style, we should acknowledge that the reality on the ground looks considerably more complex. Even individual texts contain quite a bit of variation in style. Not every Henry James sentence contains a hundred words, and not every Hemingway sentence has just ten (one in *The Green Hills of Africa* contains 424). Still, as a general system for classifying styles, the tripartite division is very useful.

Readability

Another way to think about levels of style is READABILITY, the ease with which a text can be read. Readability is of special interest to educators, publishers, and advertisers. Researchers have been studying readability since the late 1800s, and they have developed different formulas for determining a text's level of difficulty. Although they differ on details, the major studies agree that the primary indicators of a text's level of difficulty are the length and complexity of its vocabulary and sentences; long sentences and unusual words make texts hard to decipher.

Readability tests typically express a text's difficulty in terms of its grade level. For instance, according to the widely used Flesch-Kincaid Grade Level Formula, Herman Melville's *Moby Dick* is at 10th grade reading level.

Computers have proven very helpful in assessing texts' readability. Today most word processors have built-in tools that allow writers to check a document's most basic readability statistics, such as its average number of words per sentence and average word length. Various online text-analysis tools such as those provided at www.checktext.org provide far more in-depth information, calculating different readability scores for either short passages or entire works. Because they do use different factors and formulas for computing readability, these scores may vary considerably. Existing readability test are far from perfect. The Flesch-Kincaid test, for example, measures only two factors, syllables per word and sentence length; using this approach, *trochee* (two syllables) is considered an easier word than *impossible* (four), a dubious assumption. However, readability tests have grown increasingly sophisticated and accurate over the past two decades, and they will no doubt continue to do so.

Kinds of sentences

We can also characterize a style by the kinds of clauses it contains. Literary critics often label writing as either *paratactic* (from Greek "placing side by side") or *hypotactic* ("placing underneath"). A HYPOTACTIC (or SUBORDINATING) STYLE uses subordinate clauses – especially adverbial clauses – to establish relationships in time, place, or logic between one idea and the next, while a PARATACTIC (or ADDITIVE) STYLE avoids subordination.

Perhaps the most famous examples of parataxis in English come from the Bible. Here is how the English Standard Version translates Mark 4:36-41, in which Jesus stills a storm that arises while he and disciples are crossing the Sea of Galilee in a boat: *And leaving the crowd, they took him with them in the boat, just as he was. And other boats were with him. And a great windstorm arose, and the waves were breaking into the boat, so that the boat was already filling. But he [Jesus] was in the stern, asleep on the cushion. And they woke him and said to him, "Teacher, do you not care that we are perishing?" And he awoke and rebuked the wind and said to the sea, "Peace! Be still!" And the wind ceased, and there was a great calm.* These sentences are largely strung together with coordinating conjunctions: *And leaving the crowd ... And other boats were with him ... And a great wind storm arose ... But he was in the stern ... And they awoke him ... And he awoke ... And the wind ceased.* (This translation mirrors the language of the ancient Greek text.)

A hypotactic version of the same passage might begin like this: *<u>After</u> leaving the crowd, they took him with them in their boat, just as he was, <u>although</u> there were other boats as well. <u>As</u> they sailed across the sea, a great windstorm arose, causing the waves to break into the boat, so that it filled with water. <u>Since</u> Jesus was in the stern, asleep on the cushion, the disciples awoke him,* and so on. The underlined adverbial conjuncts, added in this more hypotactic version, guide the reader's understanding of the text by making more explicit how ideas relate to one another.

Another system for categorizing different kinds of clauses distinguishes between *simple, compound, complex,* and *compound-complex sentences.* A sentence that has only one independent clauses is said to be SIMPLE; one composed of two or more independent clauses is COMPOUND; a sentence containing one independent and one dependent clause is COMPLEX; and one with at least two independent clauses and at least one dependent clause is COMPOUND-COMPLEX. As their names imply, these categories are arranged in an increasing order of complexity, going from "simple" all the way to "compound-complex."

Readability versus comprehension

COMPREHENSION entails correctly interpreting the intended meaning of a text. A readable text is not necessarily an easily comprehensible one. For instance, *I read Finnegan's Wake. I don't like stream-of-consciousness narratives* is more readable than *I read Finnegan's Wake although I don't like stream-of-consciousness narratives*. The two-sentence version has more words per sentence than the one-sentence version, and, as mentioned above, sentence length is the key syntactic metric for readability. (Longer sentences put a greater burden on the reader's short-term memory.) However, the one-sentence version is easier to comprehend because it does not make the reader guess about how the information in the two clauses is related. Thus, a passage composed of simple and compound sentences is not always easier to comprehend than one consisting of complex and compound-complex sentences.

A note on usage

Many rules to good style are couched in terms of do's and (especially) don't's: don't use contractions, don't use the first person, be concise, prefer plain words to ornate ones, don't use the passive voice, and so on. As mentioned in chapter 1, such an approach is the hallmark of the prescriptive tradition. Its goal is to get students to write competently in the middle style, avoiding both the colloquialisms of the low style (such as contractions and first-person pronouns) and the excesses of the high (verbosity and ostentation).

However, as mentioned above, even in classical antiquity – when the grand style was valued more highly than today – the greatest authors displayed a mastery of all three styles. In this context, the principle of APPROPRIATENESS (or DECORUM) applies: there is no single best style, only the best style for a particular context. To use a clothing analogy, there are times to wear a tuxedo, times to wear "business casual," and times to wear sweatpants; wearing sweatpants when a tuxedo is called for is a fashion faux pas, but so is wearing a tuxedo when sweatpants are called for. Similarly, effective writers do not simply banish contractions, first-person pronouns, and passive constructions from their prose; they use them when appropriate. In terms of syntax, when writing an academic essay, compound-complex sentences are perfectly acceptable, as are sentence fragments in advertising copy.

Terms, Questions, and Exercises

STYLE, HIGH (GRAND) STYLE, MIDDLE STYLE, LOW (PLAIN) STYLE, READABILITY, HYPOTACTIC (SUBORDINATING) STYLE, PARATACTIC (ADDITIVE) STYLE, SIMPLE SENTENCE, COMPOUND SENTENCE, COMPLEX SENTENCE, COMPOUND-COMPLEX SENTENCE, COMPREHENSION, APPROPRIATENESS (DECORUM).

1. Identify the stylistic register (high, middle, or low) for each of the following passages:

    a) Good copywriters don't use fancy words. They talk like your neighbor. Or your favorite uncle.

    b) The mind is in a sad state when Sleep, the all-involving, cannot confine her spectres within the dim region of her sway, but suffers them to break forth, affrighting this actual life with secrets that perchance belong to a deeper one. (Nathaniel Hawthorne, "The Birthmark," 1843)

    c) Vigorous writing is concise. A sentence should contain no unnecessary words, a paragraph no unnecessary sentences, for the same reason that a drawing should have no unnecessary lines and a machine no unnecessary parts. (William Strunk, *The Elements of Style*, 1st edition, 1920).

2. Identify the style of the following passages as hypotactic (subordinating) or paratactic (additive):

   a) Alice was not a bit hurt, and she jumped up on to her feet in a moment: she looked up, but it was all dark overhead; before her was another long passage, and the White Rabbit was still in sight, hurrying down it. There was not a moment to be lost: away went Alice like the wind, and was just in time to hear it say, as it turned a corner, "Oh my ears and whiskers, how late it's getting!" (Lewis Carroll, *Alice's Adventures in Wonderland*, 1865.)

   b) When the people of America reflect that they are now called upon to decide a question, which, in its consequences, must prove one of the most important that ever engaged their attention, the propriety of their taking a very comprehensive, as well as a very serious, view of it will be evident. Nothing is more certain than the indispensable necessity of government, and it is equally undeniable, that whenever and however it is instituted, the people must cede to it some of their natural rights in order to vest it with requisite powers. (John Jay, *The Federalist Papers #2*, 1787.)

   c) I remained standing knee-deep in the heather, staring at the mound that hid [the Martians]. I was a battleground of fear and curiosity. I did not dare to go back towards the pit, but I felt a passionate longing to peer into it. (H. G. Wells, *The War of the Worlds*, 1898)

3. [Challenge.] The grade level assigned by readability tests indicates the years of education required to read a text. For instances, a reading level of 8 means that a text is appropriate reading for an eighth grader. Because they use different formulas, however, the tests can produce

quite different grade levels for a text. The Coleman-Liau index uses the following formula: Grade level = (average characters per word × 5.89) - (average sentences per word × 30) - 15.8. The Flesch-Kincaid readability test uses the following formula: Grade level = (average syllables per word × 11.8) + (average words per sentence × 0.39) - 15.59.

For the passages in exercise 2 above, here are the scores produced by the two readability tests (CL = Coleman-Liau; FK = Flesch-Kincaid):

a. *Alice in Wonderland*: CL = 5; FK = 14.

b. *The Federalist Papers #2*: CL = 11; FK = 22.

c. *The War of the Worlds*: CL = 6; FK = 6.

For each passage, which readability test gives the more accurate assessment? What might account for the wide variation in reading levels produced by the two tests for certain passages (2a, 2b) but not others (2c)?

(For more about readability tests, or to run various readability tests on passages of your own, you can visit http://www.checktext.org or http://www. readabilityformulas.com.)

29. Some Principles of Style

As noted in the previous chapter, the concept of *appropriateness* suggests that there is no such thing as the best style, only the best style for a particular context. However, effective writing in all three modes – the grand, the middle, and the plain – does share certain characteristics. To fully describe these characteristics would require a separate book, so we will discuss only two basic and important principles: consistency and variety. Jonathan Swift famously defined good style as "proper words in proper places." *Proper words* refers to vocabulary and *proper places* to sentence structure. Since this book is concerned with grammar, our discussion of these two principles will focus upon the latter.

Consistency

In style, CONSISTENCY means doing the same thing in the same way. Keeping an essay or story unified in subject matter, structure, and tone is fundamental to effective writing. The same also applies to grammar. For instance, the verb tense in a passage should not shift without reason. In *Genghis Khan is born in 1162 and founded the Mongol empire by the time he died*, the switch from present tense (*is born*) to past (*founded*) creates a stylistic discontinuity. The human mind has a strong desire for symmetry, and all symmetry derives from repetition.

Rhetoric in the classical tradition places great emphasis upon the practice of using repetition to create symmetrical patterns. The different kinds of repetition are called *schemes* (from Latin *schema*, "form," "figure"). Renaissance textbooks of rhetoric and composition routinely catalogued around 200 different kinds of rhetorical schemes, and typical schoolroom exercises had students practice incorporating these into their writing. Schemes were considered literary ornaments; as such, they were closely associated with the grand style, and some of the more outlandish ones – including such gems as *anantapodoton* and *bomphiologia* – are apt to strike the modern reader as extremely artificial. However, the two most basic schemes – *parallelism* and *antithesis* – can be applied in any piece of writing.

PARALLELISM is the use of grammatically identical or similar structures to describe related ideas. As a rule of thumb, the shorter the structure, the more exact the parallelism should be. For instance, a sentence such as *She likes reading manga and to draw tsundere characters* contains two non-finite nominal verb phrases, *reading manga* and *to draw tsundere characters*. When possible, it is best to keep such short structures exactly parallel: *She likes reading manga and drawing tsundere characters* or *She likes to read manga and to draw tsundere characters*. Parallelism can also extend to semantics. For instance, *They enjoy thrillers, movies with lots of body humor, and science fiction films* contains three noun phrases, but two of these are specific terms for movie genres – *thrillers* and *science fiction films* – whereas the middle term is not: *movies with lots of body humor*. A genre term for the latter would be "slapstick comedies." Therefore, a better version of the sentence would be, *They enjoy thrillers, slapstick comedies, and science fiction films*. To develop proficiency with parallelism, it is a good idea to practice keeping elements precisely alike.

Once you have mastered these simpler forms of parallelism, you can try your hand at more sophisticated kinds. Adding rhyme or other sound effects – such as alliteration, the repetition of initial sounds – can spice things up. *I came, I saw, I conquered* is memorable in English, but it sounds even better in Caesar's Latin: *Veni, vidi, vici* repeats both initial *v-* and terminal *-i*. The saying *You snooze, you lose* is memorable because of its terseness and rhyme (*snooze, lose*). More extensive instances of parallelism can also be enlivened by controlled deviations from the pattern; these often occur in the third item. A famous example occurs in the preamble to the Declaration of Independence: *We hold these truths to be self-evident, that all men are created equal, that they are endowed by their Creator with certain unalienable rights, that among these are life, liberty and the pursuit of happiness.* This sentence contains two sets of parallel structures: the three clauses beginning with *that* and, nestled within the last of these, the three noun phrases *life*, *liberty*, and *the pursuit of happiness*. In both cases, Jefferson begins with two very similar elements; *life* and *liberty* are obviously parallel, and *all men are created equal* and *they are endowed by their Creator with certain unalienable rights* are both passive clauses in which "all men" are acted upon by a cosmic force, with *created* echoed by *endowed by a Creator*. The third and final term in each, however, keeps the parallelism from getting repetitive by ringing small changes on the pattern. *Life, liberty, and the pursuit of happiness* sounds better than *life, liberty, and agency*; moreover, because *pursuit* is a noun, it also preserves the parallelism, whereas *life, liberty, and pursuing one's happiness* would not.

Parallelism is often used in ANTITHESIS, the juxtaposition of contrasting ideas. The proverb *Fool me once, shame on you; fool me twice, shame on me* is a good example. It employs both repetition and contrast, with the *shame on you – shame on me* driving home the point that only a fool falls for the same trick twice. A famous literary example of extended antithesis comes from the opening of *A Tale of Two Cities*: *It was the best of times, it was the worst of times, it was the age of wisdom, it was the age of foolishness, it was the epoch of belief, it was the epoch of incredulity, it was the season of Light, it was the season of Darkness, it was the spring of hope, it was the winter of despair, we had everything before us, we had nothing before us, we were all going direct to Heaven, we were all going direct the other way – in short, the period was so far like the present period, that some of its noisiest authorities insisted on its being received, for good or for evil, in the superlative degree of comparison only.* Each pair of clauses contains parallel constructions that drive home an essential contrast, as in *best of times, worst of times* or *age of wisdom, age of foolishness*. Without parallelism, the passage would lose its effectiveness: *It was the best of times, it was a time when many bad things occurred, it was the age of wisdom, during this period there were many foolish beliefs and practices*, and so on. Notice also that Dickens varies the basic pattern by switching from *It was* to *We had/were*, and the nouns expressing chronological reference change in each pair of clauses: *time, age, epoch, season, Spring/Winter*. These and other variations keep the parallel structures from becoming too repetitive.

Variety

Consistency helps the writer to create a well-patterned text which readers will find easy to follow, but too much repetition and regularity can easily lead to tedium; thus, consistency must be paired a counter-balancing principle: *variety*. In this context, VARIETY means controlled deviations from an established pattern to prevent monotony. Just as writers like Dickens and Jefferson prevent parallel structures from becoming too repetitive by introducing controlled variation, the same principle applies on a larger scale. The trick is to switch things up enough to provide variety, but not so much as to disrupt continuity. This can be accomplished aspects by varying *sentence length* and *sentence structure*.

Of these two, sentence length is the more easily measured indicator of syntactic variety. As mentioned in the previous chapter, most word processors have a "document properties" feature that provides an analysis of a text's sentence length. A few mouse-clicks suffice to tell me, for example, that the current chapter has (so far) 73 sentences and 1,719 words, meaning that the average sentence contains about 23 words. These figures do not tell the whole story; a text with the same statistics could have 73 sentences with 23 words each – or it could have 72 sentences with one word each, and one with 1,647. Thus, it is a good idea to count the words in individual sentences and to avoid runs of sentences with roughly the same number of words; the occasional shorter or longer sentence keeps things interesting. Paying attention to sentence length as you write will quickly become second nature, with the process of actually counting individual words soon giving way to an intuitive awareness of a passage's rhythm.

Length alone does not tell the whole story of how a sentence is built. It's true that the opening of *A Tale of Two Cities* is very long – 119 words – but these 119 words are arranged in a series of short and straight-forward parallel clauses, like *It was the best of times* and *It was the worst of times*, that are individually easy to comprehend. Compare this with the following sentence from the first chapter of Henry James' *The Ambassadors*, which contains just twelve more words than Dickens's: *There were people on the ship with whom he had easily consorted – so far as ease could up to now be imputed to him – and who for the most part plunged straight into the current that set from the landing-stage to London; there were others who had invited him to a tryst at the inn and had even invoked his aid for a "look round" at the beauties of Liverpool; but he had stolen away from every one alike, had kept no appointment and renewed no acquaintance, had been indifferently aware of the number of persons who esteemed themselves fortunate in being, unlike himself, "met," and had even independently, unsociably, alone, without encounter or relapse and by mere quiet evasion, given his afternoon and evening to the immediate and the sensible.* Unlike the opening of *A Tale of Two Cities*, this sentence is very difficult to follow. It is filled with subordinate clauses, particularly relative clauses: *with whom he had easily consorted, who for the most part plunged straight into the current, that set from the landing stage, who had invited him, [who had] invoked his aid, who esteemed themselves fortunate.* For most readers, it would take more than one reading of this sentence to be able to summarize it: "Although he'd gotten to know many people on the ship and in the hotel, he did not feel like accompanying any of them to London or Liverpool." While the sentences from *A Tale of Two Cities* and *The Ambassadors* are about the same length, they differ greatly in nature.

Thus, while it helps to change up sentence length, it is even more important to vary sentence structure. In this context, sentence structure consists of two things: the *kinds* of elements present and their *arrangement*. We can think about kinds of elements – the constituents of a sentence – at the three different levels that reflect the basic hierarchy of syntax: clauses, phrases, and words. At each level, variation comes from employing different types and sub-types of each particular structure. For instance, clauses can be dependent or independent, and dependent clauses can be nominal, adjectival, or adverbial. The arrangement of elements simply refers to the order in which they are presented. Every constituent has a normal or "default" position; thus, varying the structure of a sentence can also be achieved by moving a structure out of its accustomed place.

In practice, it is easiest to achieve varied syntax by focusing on the level of the phrase. In part two of this book, we learned about the five major kinds of phrases – noun phrases, verb phrases, adjective phrases, adverb phrases, and prepositional phrases – as well as the three kinds of non-finite verb phrases, present participle phrases, past participle phrases, and infinitive phrases; furthermore, verb phrases have five basic patterns of complementation. Varying sentence structure simply means not repeating the same kinds of phrases over and over, especially in the same order. Consider the following excerpt from a student essay: *The story of Sir Gawain and the Green Knight is a tale that embodies many of the defining characteristics of the quest archetype. One of these aspects in the tale is the Call to Adventure.* Both sentences use the basic structure NP – *is* – NP: *The story is a tale* and *One [aspect] is the Call to Adventure.* Moreover, in just two brief sentences, the writer uses five prepositional phrases, four of them headed by *of*. A less repetitive version of these sentences might read: *Sir Gawain and the Green Knight embodies many of the quest archetype's defining characteristics, including the Call to Adventure.*

A note on usage

One of the most common rhetorical schemes in proverbs and other pithy expressions is CHIASMUS, wherein two parallel clauses repeat words in reverse order (*abba*). Well-known examples include *The last [a] shall be first [b], and the first [b] last [a]* (*The Gospel of Matthew*), *All [a] for one [b] and one [b] for all [a]* (Alexandre Dumas, *The Three Musketeers*), and *People don't care [a] how much you know [b] until they know [b] how much you care [a]* (attributed to Theodore Roosevelt).

Terms, Questions, and Exercises

CONSISTENCY, PARALLELISM, ANTITHESIS, VARIETY, CHIASMUS.

1. Revise the sentences below for more effective parallelism, keeping the elements as closely parallel as possible:

   a) I enjoy soccer, tennis, and playing golf.

   b) You can judge people by their actions or by what they say.

   c) Nikola Tesla claimed that his "death beam" could destroy any object within two hundred miles, and entire cities could be enclosed behind an invulnerable curtain of power.

2. Revise the sentences below for more effective antithesis:

   a) I love pizza, but I strongly dislike eating cauliflower.

   b) Some people cheered, and then there others who were booing.

   c) The magazine article claims that the Internet makes us dumber, but, according to other experts, our intelligence has been increased by the web.

3. One way to achieve variety in sentence length is through sentence combining. Combine each of the sentence pairs below into one longer sentence:

   a) The first modern printing press was invented by Johannes Gutenberg. Gutenberg was a goldsmith and entrepreneur from the city of Mainz.

   b) Mainz was the capital of Germany's Rhineland-Palatinate. Mainz was part of the Holy Roman Empire.

   c) Gutenberg applied his skill in metalworking to a number of different business ventures. In 1439, he borrowed money to manufacture special mirrors for capturing "holy light" from religious relics.

4. List three examples of chiasmus other than the ones mentioned in this chapter. (You can find quotes or invent them yourself.)

30. Part 3 Review

Chapter 20 Terms
DECLARATIVE CLAUSE, IMPERATIVE CLAUSE, LET-IMPERATIVE, DO-IMPERATIVE, OPEN INTERROGATIVE CLAUSE, CLOSED INTERROGATIVE CLAUSE, GAP, EXCLAMATORY CLAUSE.

Chapter 21 Terms
COORDINATION, COORDINATE STRUCTURES, CONJUNCTS, NEGATION, SERIAL COMMA.

Chapter 22 Terms
MATRIX CLAUSE, CONTENT CLAUSE, SUBORDINATE DECLARATIVE CONTENT CLAUSE, SUBORDINATE INTERROGATIVE CONTENT CLAUSE, CLOSED INTERROGATIVE CONTENT CLAUSE, OPEN INTERROGATIVE CONTENT CLAUSE, SUBORDINATE EXCLAMATORY CONTENT CLAUSE.

Chapter 23 Terms
RELATIVE CLAUSE, RESTRICTIVE (DEFINING) RELATIVE CLAUSE, NON-RESTRICTIVE (NON-DEFINING RELATIVE CLAUSE).

Chapter 24 Terms
ADVERBIAL SUBORDINATE CLAUSE.

Chapter 25 Terms
ELLIPSIS, CLAUSE OF COMPARISON.

Chapter 26 Terms

MOVEMENT, SEMANTIC MOVEMENT, SYNTACTIC MOVEMENT, SUBJUNCTIVE MOOD, INDICATIVE MOOD, IMPERATIVE MOOD.

Chapter 27 Terms

PUNCTUATION, SENTENCE, PERIOD, COLON, SEMI-COLON, COMMA, DASH, APOSTROPHE, SENTENCE FRAGMENT, COMMA SPLICE.

Chapter 28 Terms

STYLE, HIGH (GRAND) STYLE, MIDDLE STYLE, LOW (PLAIN) STYLE, READABILITY, HYPOTACTIC (SUBORDINATING) STYLE, PARATACTIC (ADDITIVE) STYLE, SIMPLE SENTENCE, COMPOUND SENTENCE, COMPLEX SENTENCE, COMPOUND-COMPLEX SENTENCE, COMPREHENSION, APPROPRIATENESS (DECORUM).

Chapter 29 Terms

CONSISTENCY, PARALLELISM, ANTITHESIS, VARIETY, CHIASMUS.

1. Give an example of an open interrogative clause. How are these clauses formed?

2. Give an example of an closed interrogative clause. How are these clauses formed?

3. Rephrase the closed interrogative clauses below so that each is declarative, omitting *do*. (Example: *Do you like apple pie? – You like apple pie.*)

    a) Will you read Chaucer's "Knight's Tale" for next class?

    b) Did he lock his keys in the car?

    c) Might Halley's comet return in 2061?

4. Rephrase the interrogative clauses below so that each is declarative, substituting the appropriate indefinite pronoun for the interrogative word. As above, omit *do*. To

recall, the corresponding word pairs are *who/whom –
someone, what – something, when – sometime (or: at some
time), whose – someone's, which – some, where – somewhere, how – somehow, why – for some reason*. (Example:
*When did she start jogging? – She started jogging at some
time*.)

    a) Who holds the world's record in the long jump?

    b) For whom did you buy those flowers?

    c) Why did he return the pair of black shoes to the
store?

5. Imperative clauses are formed with the _____ form of a
verb.

6. Does the sentence *This is such a cozy chair!* contain an
exclamatory clause? Why or why not?

7. Name the coordinate structures in the sentences below
and identify their function. If there are none, write "none."
(Example: *The weather was unseasonably cold and rainy.
– unseasonably cold* and *rainy* are coordinate adjective
phrases.)

    a) More and more suburban residents rent their homes.

    b) Somewhere men are laughing, and somewhere chil-
dren shout, but there is no joy in Mudville—for
mighty Casey struck out. (From "Casey at the Bat,"
with slight modifications.)

    c) [Challenge.] The disc was scratched and cracked, so
we could not watch the movie.

8. What two kinds of clauses often begin with the subordinator *that*?

9. How can you distinguish between the clauses mentioned
in the previous question?

10. In the sentences below, identify any subordinate clauses, then specify the nature of the clause (content, relative, or adverbial) and its function (nominal, adjectival, or adverbial):

   a) I know that the mail will arrive late today.

   b) The novel that I just finished reading had a weak ending.

   c) For a long time, she wondered why some people drink so much coffee.

   d) Since we left early, we missed the movie's ending.

   e) Please tell me whether you're going to eat that pie.

11. In the spaces below, provide the correct form of *who* (*who*, *whom*, or *whose*):

   a) The student ____ bicycle was stolen reported the theft.

   b) We talked to the same sales representative ____ you spoke with.

   c) He ____ wants nothing has everything.

12. Punctuate the sentences listed below to make all relative clauses non-restrictive.

   a) The salsa which we sampled contained habanero peppers.

   b) The fans who did not have tickets were turned away.

   c) We saw the ship which was supposed to sail at noon.

13. Create three sentences with ellipsis, writing the omitted information in brackets. Then identify the ellipsis as required or optional.

14. True or false? In the sentence *Since that time, I have learned to be cautious*, *since that time* is an adverbial clause with an omitted verb. false

15. Correct the punctuation of the sentences below. (If they are already correctly punctuated, write "correct.")

   a) The seemingly endless drive in the cramped car, made the first part of the trip difficult to endure.

   b) John Bunyan, author of *The Pilgrim's Progress* had little formal education. But, he wrote sixty books.

   c) In the early twentieth century many breakthroughs in physics came from scientists under 40, they picked up the theory of quantum mechanics more readily than their senior colleagues.

16. True or false? The complement of a phrase always follows the head; therefore, the direct object of a verb can never occur before the verb itself.

17. Identify the mood of the underlined verb in <u>Were</u> *he to quit now, he would waste all of his hard work.*

18. What is a comma splice? Give an example.

19. What is a sentence fragment? Give an example.

20. Using the conventions of formal written English, correct the punctuation errors in the sentences below. (If there are none, write "none.")

   a) He arrived late to the interview. Which was a big mistake.

   b) The company's two representatives, were just about to leave when he arrived.

   c) He claimed the interview was scheduled for a later time, they did not believe him. Although, they went ahead with the interview anyway.

21. What is the difference between a paratactic and a hypotactic style?

22. What are the characteristics of the low, middle, and high styles? What are some potential benefits and drawbacks of each? In what contexts might a writer employ the different styles?

23. How does readability differ from comprehensibility?

24. Revise the sentences below for more effective parallelism or antithesis, keeping the elements as closely parallel as possible:

    a) In the Wars of the Roses, the House of York descended from Edmund Langley, Duke of York, while John of Gaunt, the Duke of Lancaster, founded the House of Lancaster.

    b) Edmund and John were brothers, but a bitter rivalry came about between their descendants.

    c) The Yorkists won the vast majority of battles – including First St. Albans, Towton, and the Battle of Tewkesbury – but the final, decisive battle, Bosworth Field, was one they lost.

25. What are some ways that writers can enhance "vanilla" parallelism to make it more effective and/or memorable?

Made in the USA
Lexington, KY
07 January 2018